SALT
THE FIFTH ELEMENT

*The sacredness and dignity of salt!
This mineral is like unto the four elements—earth, air, fire and water. So
universal, so necessary to life, it is the
fifth element.*
JEAN DE MARCOUNILLE
Paris, 1584.

SALT
THE FIFTH ELEMENT

The Story of a Basic
American Industry

BY

GARNETT LAIDLAW ESKEW

Author of
The Pageant of The Packets—A Book of American Steamboating:
The Lightning Line: Twin Ribbons of Singing Steel, etc.

ILLUSTRATED BY MARY CONSTANCE ENSLOW

CHICAGO
'J. G. FERGUSON AND ASSOCIATES
1948

To

STERLING MORTON

CONTENTS

Part One

Part Two

x

ILLUSTRATIONS

Additional photographic illustrations shown in groups

INTRODUCTION

I T WAS LONG a characteristic of us Americans to accept the
commonplace material advantages we enjoy, without question as to who and what have been responsible for our having
them. Recently, however, a change has come about. The dissolution of many weaker nations overseas, the rise of the Power
State and the accompanying disappearance of the rights and com-
forts of the individual have caused many of us to inquire for the
first time:

How is it that we have this or that? What is the story behind
the growth of one or another of the great American industries?
And, since we are told again and again that the accomplishment
is but the extended shadow of some man or men, who are the men
who have made possible the good things we have whose sum total
so greatly adds, in a material sense, to what we know as the
American way of life?

To answer these questions, publishers have wisely begun to
put out a gratifying array of factual books. True, the stories are
often clothed in fictionized or dramatized garments; yet they are
nonetheless authentic. In the book stalls and the libraries you
will find stories of our great railroad lines; of the motor car, the
telegraph, the telephone; of the sugar, the rubber, the oil industries, and of any number of other lines of endeavor. And
behind each and every one, the dominant, driving personalities
which have made that particular industry great.

It happens that I grew up in a one time salt-producing region
and often thought about the American salt industry. But when I
went to look for published books on the subject I found none—
none, that is, save some technical treatises and a few pamphlets
of a commercial or industrial sort, not to mention local histories
and a valuable book or two on some specific phase of salt. There
was nothing about the growth of the industry per se or of the men
who made it. No one apparently had thought it worth while to

dig out and assemble the facts essential to such a story. Salt, you see, is one of those simple, undramatic, matter-of-course items which we accept. Period.

This dearth of salt books induced me in time to write a book on the subject. For facts, I turned to the archives of the Morton Salt Company, only producer operating in all the Nation's major salt fields. That Company was just on the point of celebrating its 100th. anniversary, and therefore had a gratifying mass of facts about salt already assembled.

Talks with the heads of the Company led me to take a "swing around the circuit" of the various Morton operations. First, though, I went to Syracuse, New York, the once "salt city" of early America. Then back to my native Kanawha Valley where, three-quarters of a century before, my forebears had made salt and where local histories yielded a good record of a vanished trade. Next, to the plains of Kansas; to the shores of Lake Michigan; to the solar ponds of Utah and the California coast; to the mines of Texas and Louisiana and to the big plant of Worcester Salt Company, at Silver Springs, New York.

Information gathered from all of these various salt-making operations, past and present, bolstered by historical and industrial material obtained by research, forms the basis of this volume. In no sense is it intended to be a history of salt: one does not encompass a subject as old as the human race itself in the scope of one brief volume. I intend it to be simply a book about salt, from the reading of which one may better understand another of our Nation's great enterprises upon which we depend, and the men who have made it.

Garnett Laidlaw Eskew

Washington, D. C.

1 March, 1948

SALT

PART ONE

CHAPTER ONE

THE *WHY* OF THIS BOOK

ACROSS THE RETINA of my boyhood's imagination moved a long procession of loaded salt boats, endlessly floating. Not that I ever actually saw them; the salt industry in our Valley, of which those boats were an essential part, ended many years before I made my entry into the world. But the picture was there nevertheless. I learned about the boats and the cargo they carried from the men who had seen them, owned them, worked them, loaded them. It had all happened in the days when the salt furnaces had flourished in our Valley . . . .

Forty-six furnaces strung out along a river within the short space of ten miles. A continual cloud of smoke pouring from their fat, high chimneys. Mountains of white salt in the sheds,

1

growing with the passing days until, the salt having properly "cured" (i.e., the excess moisture having drained off), they would be torn down by husky black laborers with wide wooden shovels. Then, loaded into barrels, the salt would be rolled aboard flatboats or steamboats. Twelve hundred barrels to a boat, it would go downstream to supply the needs of Cincinnati packing houses—the needs, in fact, of a large segment of the entire Nation.

But of that once vast industry there remained, in my boyhood, but one lone furnace which produced and shipped by rail a few thousand bushels of salt where formerly the boats had taken out millions.

Our Valley is a long and slender strip of low ground in West Virginia, extending ninety miles between two blue, diminishing ranges of hills—foothills of the Alleghanies. It reaches from the interior of West Virginia to the Ohio River. Through it flows the Kanawha River—river of many white caps, so the Indians dubbed it for some inexplicable reason—a stream that goes alternately red-brown with winter floods and emerald in the midsummer drought; and along whose channel, time out of mind, had moved the procession of American migration from the Atlantic seaboard to the Midlands. Indian, pioneer, frontiersman, settler—one and all they had paused in our Valley on their westward trek to make salt at the "buffalo lick," where wild animals once sought to quench their hunger for salt by licking the rocks and earth over which natural brine bubbled from the earth's innards.

Taking their cue from the animals, men in time got salt there, too; and around the buffalo lick, and adjacent to it, the salt industry, as our Valley knew it, grew up.

Charleston, our home town, lies on the Kanawha's shore midway between a point where the river is born of the union of two other rivers, and another point, forty miles west, where it is caught up in the Ohio's current and borne 800 miles away to contribute its bit to the mighty Mississippi's sweep.

Charleston had been the financial capital of the Valley's salt industry, but the furnaces and the wells were located six miles away at the little town of Malden, once known as Kanawha Salines, within spitting distance of the buffalo lick. With the getting out of the salt, Malden grew, rose to prominence, became wealthy. There lived most of the salt tycoons who lined their pockets with the proceeds of the industry, employed thousands of workers, built fine homes and organized a trust—the first trust in the United States—which frankly and with intent operated in restraint of trade, but which worked mightily to their own advantage.

But as new times had come, the Valley salt industry fell upon evil days. Malden, her chief interest gone, dropped pleasantly into the status of a small town of many memories. Salt makers and their workers sought new pursuits. The boat-building craft and the cooperage trade—handmaids, both, of salt making— gave way to newer activities. Charleston far outgrew Malden. The railroads came and the salt boats rotted and sank.

The men who had made salt in their youth and who had white hair when I became old enough to know what they were talking about, used to tell me of the salty old times in the Valley. They would gather, those old fellows, evenings and Saturday afternoons, at Dr. Rogers' Drugstore on Front Street, whence they could look out at the steamboats that frequently passed. They met for no other reason in the world than to swap yarns and discuss old times and talk about the vanished trade.

Listening to them, I learned the big names among our local salt makers—Brooks, Dickinson, Hale, Ruffner, Laidley, Alderson, Clarkson, Quarrier, Smith, Shrewsbury, Tompkins—what a race of individualists they were! I heard how they sank "gums" (hollowed logs) into the mud and brought forth a steady stream of brine from a big lake or sea that (so the old men told me) underlies our whole state. . . . How they would cement together a dozen big iron kettles or pans most anywhere along the bank close to the well, put a chimney at one end and a fire-bed under the other, call it a furnace, and set her going!...How they would boil the brine until all the water was gone; barrel the remaining salt and ship it out to Porkopolis (Cincinnati to you!) and to merchants and farmers all along the rivers. Meanwhile, mountain wagons—until the railroads came—were taking care of the eastern shipments: the salt bound for Baltimore, Richmond, and Alexandria, over there east of the Alleghany and Blue Ridge barriers.

I tried to visualize it from what they told me—a self-contained, completely independent little industry that got along very well without help from any other section of the country. Right there in our Valley they fashioned the machinery, drills, kettles, everything, at local blacksmith shops. There, too, they boiled the brine, built the boats, made the barrels by hand, developed short cuts. This industry bred a race of producers who entertained not the least doubt in the world that they were the salt of the earth no less than was the stuff they sold—men of standing and wealth, when wealth was reckoned in tens of thousands rather than in millions.

I recall a day when one of the old boys pointed out a tall, shabby, weatherbeaten, dignified old man walking by the drugstore. He bowed to all, but did not stop.

"Sonny," I was told, "See that old fellow? That's Dr. Hale. Used to be the wealthiest man in these parts fifty years ago. Biggest salt maker. Head of the whole salt shebang. Wouldn't think it to look at him, would you? Well, did you know his great grandmother was the first white person to make salt in this Valley? Learned it from the Indians. Name was Mary Ingles."

Oh, yes, I knew about Mary Ingles! What child in our Valley did not? Had not Aunt Peggy, our old nurse, told it to us often, to make us behave? Mary Ingles—who had been captured by the Indians and seen her baby snatched by a painted savage and its brains knocked out against a tree because it squalled too much.

But there was one thing that I did not learn from the former salt makers. They never told me why salt making in our Valley ended; what killed it off. From their remarks I gathered that one year the salt business was going great guns; the next it was a dead pigeon in American commerce. I used to wonder about that. Did the supply of natural brine run out? I didn't see how that could be with a whole lake full of it right beneath us. From what cause then, natural or human, were the furnaces now cold and dead; the boats scuttled; the pumps stilled; the men and money diverted to other interests?

Not until years later did I take the trouble to dig up the answers to these questions. By the time I had grown up I had begun to read the record of salt in its relation to life—the part it has played in history, in religion, in national customs; the influence it has had on the Nation's settlement, in determining the course of empire and trade routes. I learned of the battles that have been waged and the blood that has been shed for the possession of the sources of it; its essentiality to the life and well-being not only of man as an individual but to men as nations; and man's unremitting effort through the ages to insure himself a constant supply of this vital element.

Then I began to realize that our Kanawha salt industry was but one milestone on the march of salt—one single operation, one step forward in the progress of producing and distributing a commodity that has become as necessary to many facets of our civilization as the air we breathe.

So far as this Nation is concerned, the struggle for salt began with the first colonists to settle the North American shores. And the intervening years have left other mileposts to show other steps in the march of salt. Syracuse, N. Y.; Saltville, Va.; Pomeroy, Ohio; Connemaugh, Pa.—all once important centers of production, but now sunk into uselessness, so far as salt production goes.

Then, too, there were the numerous "licks" or salt springs scattered through Kentucky, Ohio, Indiana and other midland states—most of which were but wayside boiling places, where battered kitchen kettles bubbled over improvised fires, and yielded a few gritty, dank, hard lumps for the moment-pausing sojourners. Others, as mentioned, became vital to the Nation's markets and produced totals which reached up into six figures, because the then conditions combined to make salt production, as practiced, a profitable and mechanically expeditious industry.

But we live in a Nation where change and progress are constantly at work. For several reasons these early salt sources had within them the seeds of their own dissolution. The matter of transportation, ease and cost of getting the salt out of the ground, refining it and distributing it to people who must have it— these had their part in developing through years of trial and error the American salt industry as we now know it—a series of strategically located plants, in various parts of the country, each equipped to serve the territory contiguous to it.

And so it was that one boy, listening to the old men's tales of one phase of American salt making, decided sometime he would tell the story of Salt. This volume is the tangible evidence that he has kept his word.

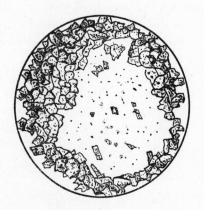

CHAPTER TWO

SALT IS WHERE YOU FIND IT

MAN EXPERIENCED his first need for salt so early in his career that there is no record of when that discovery took place.

When the curtain of recorded history rises, there we find man taking salt for his stomach's sake, seasoning his food with it, and feeding it to his animals; and doing it with the air of having been at it a long while. Not even the most astute scientist would undertake to say when man and salt first got together—or how.

Possibly it happened this way: Along certain ocean beaches people have noticed how receding tides leave a gleaming incrustation of salt in the bays and inlets. Our worthy common ancestor, Eolithic man, was attracted by such a salt pit shining there in the sunlight. Putting some of the gleaming substance to his lips, he found it had a tart, zesty, distinctive taste, absolutely unlike anything he had ever experienced before. Whereupon he put a chunk of it in his mouth and discovered immediately that too much made him sick. Taken in the right proportion, however, the stuff was pleasant.

Gathering some in his great hairy fists, he took it home to show his wife and offspring. The old lady grunted with appreciation. Rubbing it on a haunch of venison, the two made another discovery. Not only was the satisfying taste of salt there, but the taste of the meat itself was enhanced noticeably. Like the diviner's rod which came into use thousands of years later, salt had a way of revealing hidden values—taste values.

And so, before long, man was using salt gathered from the seaside in practically all his food and wondering how he had ever got along without it. For one thing, it increased his feeling of well-being. Our ancestor, in his primitive ignorance, had no way of knowing that he had all along been acquiring a certain amount of salt from the flesh of animals which he ate, they having assimilated certain quantities in their own food. But with the direct addition of salt to his diet, man was augmenting the limited supply within his system and replenishing it as it drained out of his body in the form of sweat and other excretion, and it made him feel better.

Time passed, and man, being a gregarious animal, began to gather with his fellows in groups. Finding that garnering salt from the extensive tidal residue was an unhandy business, they proceeded to build little dams of their own to imprison or block off seawater in small salt ponds. Old Sol, shining up there in the heavens then as now, dried up the water in the ponds and there on the bottom lay a nice layer of white salt. The men of the village gathered it up for their use and took it to their homes. Of course, it was pretty well mixed with sea sand. But primitive man wasn't particular; he soon learned to separate salt from sand. Thus life moved on, a pleasanter thing because of the Great Seasoner which man had found.

Not all men, of course, lived on the seacoasts. But bountiful Nature took care of that. Away from the coasts, far inland, coursing up through the then changing layers of the earth's strata, natural brine gurgled to the surface in salt springs. Around these springs inland men lived or came periodically to supply their

wants by taking the spring water and letting it evaporate in the
sun just as the coast men were doing.

And animals, too! Great, hairy creatures—long-tusked, and
sharp-fanged—which the eye of present man never sees save
in his nightmares! These came crowding and snarling and grunt-
ing around the places of salt. They drank their fill. They licked
the rocks and salty earth. They wallowed in the salt mud. In such
great numbers did they come that they often wore veritable
depressions in the earth, visible to this day. In southern Illinois
there is a great basin called the "half moon," worn out by visiting
delegations of salt-hungry mastodons, ages ago. Around these
salt springs man must have found some excellent hunting, if
we may judge by the ancient stone weapons that have been
unearthed nearby.

The very name "lick" still clings to certain of these springs.
Booneslick, Mayslick, Big Bone Lick, French Lick, Bluelick, buffalo licks and salt licks innumerable, as well as many other
kinds of licks—these are all now place names in our country's
geography. They testify to the fact that animals, too, both in
ancient and modern times sought them out for a single purpose:
to appease their natural craving for salt.

As though perfectly aware of mankind's enduring need for
salt, Nature has implanted enormous quantities of it in and over
the earth. According to estimates by people who should know,
we need never have any fear of a salt shortage, let alone a salt
famine. There is more than ample salt-in-the-rough on this
planet. It is the production and refining of that rough product
to meet the uses of our civilization's complex economy, no less
than transporting it, that present now, as in the past, the problem
of supplying all the earth's inhabitants. As we read farther in
this book we shall discover how the people of our own Nation
have met and overcome that obstacle.

The Vast Storehouses of Sea and Earth

There is a lot of salt in the sea. Says that dignified and impartial mentor, the *Encyclopaedia Britannica:* "Assuming that each gallon of water contains .2547 pounds of salt and allowing an average density of 2.24 for rock salt, it has been computed that, if dried up, the entire ocean would contain no less than 4½ million cubic miles of rock salt—or about 14½ times the bulk of the entire continent of Europe above high water."

Also, there are many inland salt lakes and seas. One of them, the Dead Sea in Asia Minor, is 340 square miles in area. It contains 11,400 million tons of salt. And the River Jordan, feeding that Biblically historic body (although if you taste the Jordan it is an apparently fresh water stream), brings down each year a little more salt, about 35 parts in 100,000, to add to its salinity. Even so, the Jordan contributes 850,000 tons of salt annually. The same fact is relatively true of all fresh-water streams. As a further illustration, our own Mississippi River brings down its sizeable bit of salt to the Mexican Gulf.

How come salt? Scientists for the most part say that it originated within the rocks in the earth. All rocks, geologically speaking, are in the process of decay due to atmospheric action. They have been decaying for millions of years. Sodium chloride (common salt) is constantly being carried away in solution by rain-water.

Into the streams and rivers it goes. Finally it reaches the sea. For ages streams have thus been carrying salt from the decaying rocks down to the ocean and to the land-locked salt-water bodies. Evaporation by the sun continually causes these salt-water bodies to deposit thick layers of salt.

But what about the millions and millions of tons that lie buried in the earth, at places fairly close to the surface? The explanation is simply that the ocean, or a section of the ocean cut off from the main body, was there at one time and deposited these mighty layers as a result of solar evaporation. Then, in the primordial geologic processes of Nature, the earth heaved and sank, was squeezed and reshaped; the sea dried up or was swept away to other parts of the globe. In time, after the passing of still other ages, the salt strata lay deep below the surface of the ground, overlaid with other and newer strata: sand, marl, shale, limestone, clay and various additional deposits.

Here is an example: A great ocean known as the Permian Sea once rolled untrammelled across parts of the present states of Kansas, Texas, Oklahoma, Colorado, and New Mexico. This fact accounts for the rich salt deposits which today are mined extensively in that area. In the same way, through north central New York State, more salt deposits were left by an arm of the sea that once swept over that area. At some places in the New York salt belt, rich artesian brines come up through salt springs (notably in the vicinity of the city of Syracuse). The brine was so strong and plentiful, moreover, that, as we shall see later on, it was utilized for many years to supply a large segment of the American nation.

In other parts of New York, in sections of Ohio, Louisiana, and Michigan, in Kansas and in Texas men have only to sink a shaft a few hundred feet to reach the salt stratum. There they find it waiting for them in the form of rock salt (known scientifically as *halite*), which can be dug and brought out by various methods for refining and distribution.

In other parts of the country great quantities of brine were occluded in sand at the time of their deposition and have remained there ever since. According to Dr. W. C. Phalen, of the U. S. Bureau of Mines, these brines may be considered as "fossil seawater." Salt reservoirs (or seas, or lakes) of this kind underlie parts of the Ohio and Kanawha River valleys in West Virginia and in eastern Ohio. These sections produce brine pumped up from wells sunk down into those subterranean lakes. As an example the Kanawha Valley, as already indicated, once ranked high as a producer of salt from such natural brine.

And then there is Great Salt Lake in Utah. It is but a puddle in comparison to the vanished sea of which it is a remnant. It is many times saltier than the ocean, as, having no outlet it constantly gathers more salt from its tributaries. Here, too, salt is today produced to supply an extensive surrounding territory.

Salt Over the World

For a small coin you can buy a good-sized can of salt in any American grocery, the United States being the world's largest producer and consumer of that product. But as you read on you will discover that it was not always plentiful here; and even yet, in many other parts of the globe there is not nearly enough salt produced to go around.

It wasn't so long ago that an Abyssinian millionaire was spoken of as "he that eateth salt". The natives in the market places of Central Africa invariably turn up their noses at trinkets and household goods, if they can get salt instead. Men have been murdered for salt. Wars have raged over it. Yet there is enough, as you may have gathered from the preceding pages, to supply every man and beast that populates all the countries of this terrestial ball, as long, probably, as the human race endures.

The Phoenicians, earliest of foreign traders, navigators par excellence, peddled salt in their open galleys to the ancient ports of the Mediterranean before the time of written history. Relics uncovered in Belgium tell a tale of cavemen using salt 5000 years ago. About 3000 years ago the ancient Trojans were eating salt fish and liking it. The early Egyptians employed salt in behalf of both the living and the dead; to season food for, and revivify, the former; to embalm the latter.

"Royal decree!" shouted the heralds of the Chinese Emperor Yu in the province of Shantung about 2000 B. C. "My loyal subjects will keep my court supplied with salt!" They had their own peculiar way of getting it, those ancient Chinese. They took seaweed from the briny deep, dried, boiled it and evaporated the juice.... If you have ever smelled seaweed drying, you may imagine the taste of that early Chinese salt.

The spreading demand for it made salt, in time, an industry. Men went into the business of producing and supplying towns or regions. No one knows when that began. The salt industry may have had its birth prehistorically in Palestine, the same country whence sprang the Christian religion. For there was located the Dead Sea whose waters are many times saltier than the ocean. It has yielded salt for men from time immemorial, and still yields it.

Historians, however, can say with certainty that the first industrial salt production of which they have positive record occurred in Italy. The long boot is completely seagirt, save across its top. It was very natural for those who dwelt along Italy's vast coastline to turn to the sea for salt, even as they did for fish. It is recorded that Ancus Martius, fourth of the early Roman kings, began the industrial production of salt by letting the sea into an enclosed basin.

One gains a realizing sense of salt's importance to early Rome when he recalls that the Via Salaria, at this moment an important thoroughfare in the modern Italian capital, was built by Roman soldiers long before the Christian era to bear caravans of salt from the works at Ostia to supply the then world metropolis. The almost noiseless pad of camel's feet, the *plop-plop* of plodding asses' hooves, the shouts of drivers, the slow rattle of solid-wheel ox carts, the rhythmic tramp of Roman guards, the creaking of chariot wheels—one can in his mind's eye view the passing show on that ancient Via Salaria: salt moving into town and merchandise moving out again to barter for more salt.

So valuable a commodity was subject at any time to attack by robbers or by some of Rome's enemy forces. Hence a heavy constabulary stood guard always along Via Salaria. At that time the Roman government paid off its soldiers in the very stuff they protected—salt. From which fact we derive our word *sal-*

*Citizens of Verona, Italy, had to get salt through rationing boards
in the 14th Century*

ary. If one of the guardsmen along Via Salaria did not do his job right, he was said "not to be worth his salt," just as we say today of a lazy, trifling workman.

Setting out from Rome with all the customary fanfare and panoply which attended his going to the wars, Julius Caesar carried along with his farriers, blacksmiths, and carpenters, a number of "salinators"—men who would make salt in the countries of barbaric northern Europe toward which he was bound for conquest.

All Italy, down into medieval times, made salt a veritable contraband. The Englishman Locke visited Venice in 1553 and noted the current legislation regarding salt. "Neither may any man in Venice buy more salt than he spendeth in the city," Locke complains indignantly, "for if he be known to carie one ounce out of the city, and be accused therefor, he loseth an ear!"

The spotlight of history moved from Italy up through Europe, salt retaining its importance in the life of man. Very early there were salt works on the French coast; at Halles in Germany; at Wieliczka in Poland. "These German tribes!" exclaimed Tacitus in disgust, in the third century. "These Chatti and Hermanduri! They fight bloody wars over who shall possess a salt 'stream'." Russia has, within her boundaries, salt enough to supply all Europe. Both Russia and Spain have hills of salt.

The mighty salt mine at Wieliczka, Poland, is still operating. Rock salt has been mined there for nearly 1000 years. In 1939, the Germans, invading Poland's territory, made a beeline for Crakow near which the salt mine is located. For some reason, they did not destroy its miles of subterranean hallways containing chapels, music and dance halls, innumerable examples of the sculptor's art—all done in natural rock salt. Since the end of the war Poland has taken over and Wieliczka has gone to work again for Poland.

Nearby, other rock salt mines used to be worked by convict labor, an inhuman procedure under even the best conditions. And the conditions were definitely not best in this instance.

How salt miners worked in a medieval European mine

These workmen, it must be admitted, were among the country's worst criminals. Frequently they rose and fought to make a dash for their freedom. Once, long ago, according to some old records, they staged a sit-down strike in the mine. Refused absolutely to leave it. Whereupon the guards simply walked out and left them with plenty of salt and not a drop of water. That brought the workers to time. But the uprisings came along in such quick succession that the guard was trebled, and at every shouted order, all workmen in the salt mine were trained to fall flat upon their faces.

There are plenty of salt springs in Austria. In the neighborhood of Hitler's home, Berchtesgaden, there was once a famous salt mine. Germany rose to great importance as a world power on her natural resources, salt among them. Wide and thick and rich, her salt strata extend beneath the country. Its many active mines furnished an essential of chemical warfare, as well as of the vast pre-war German chemical industry.

"Passersby, here you behold the mortal remains of a pig which acquired for itself imperishable glory through the discovery of the salt spring of Luneburg." So reads an inscription on a glass case before the town hall of that old German city. Inside are the shriveled remains of a once fat porker.

Holland early developed meat and fish curing with salt obtained by windmill-and-seawater combination. There was a law in Holland several centuries ago that if a citizen used inferior salt to dry herring, that citizen forfeited his fish-curing rights.

The French people are supposed to have learned salt making from the Romans. Early solar salt plants in Lorraine date back to the Caesars' time. So productive were they that in 1334 salt making was put under state control by Phillipe VI and a heavy duty imposed. La Gabelle, so the people called this law; and its oppressive provisions and inordinately heavy fines which included life imprisonment and fifteen years at the galleys did nothing to make the peasants love their king better. Continuing through various reigns this tax added fuel to the flame of French revolution.

Coming down to the present, some scientists ascribe the constantly falling birth rate in modern France to the high taxes on salt. Professor Babcock, famous dairying expert, has proved that cattle deprived of salt or getting insufficient salt in their diet, do not have as many or as healthy calves as they should, and finally become sterile. The same condition may apply to the French people.

A—Sea. B—Pool. C—Gate. D—Trenches. E—Salt basins. F—Rake. G—Shovel.

Medieval artist's conception of salt making

Struggle for Tax-Free Salt

Where did Americans get their well-known "Yankee ingenuity"? From the English? Possibly. For when Julius Caesar landed in 55 BC with his army to conquer the land and show the backward inhabitants how to build roads and make salt, he brought salinators along to show them the latter trick. He found, however, that the Britons already knew it. They were getting their supply—God save us!—by pouring brine over hot faggots and then scraping off the crust for general use.

"Let my salinators show you a better way than that!" said the great contemptuous Roman to the men of Cheshire. The Romans had open pans and in these they boiled brine over open fires. The result was so satisfactory that the Cheshiremen for the next 1700 years made salt just that way, with successive improvements as time went on, of course.

Many years later William the Conqueror, before he crossed the channel, sent to inquire into the salt situation in England. Should he bring his own supply?

"Not necessary," the spies reported. "These English boil their pans fifteen times and make a whole horse-load."

A place where salt was made was known as a "wich" in Anglo Saxon, a fact which has named many an English town—Greenwich, Ipswich, Sandwich, etc., and there was an old law requiring "whoever loads his wain so that the axle breaks within two leagues of any wich, pays the King's Officer two shillings, if overtaken."

The Conqueror kept Droitwich as his own little royal demesne because of its rich salt yield. Under direct supervision of the King, the salt area was parcelled out to his favorites. There were, however, certain regulations which even the favorites had to abide by in order to insure distribution.

Some day when you are reading through the Domesday Book—that ancient gloomy-sounding record of Norman England—you may chance upon this bit of information: "Walling" salt meant simply making salt. A man who was "occupying walling" was enjoying the right to make salt from natural brine by the King's favor. And it was a right very highly prized, let me tell you!

In medieval England salt continued an item of high importance, recognized as a dividing line at the dinner table. A host, if noble, would place his guests "above or below the salt," according to their rank—those sitting above being closer to nobility (himself) , than those below.

What happened when Royalty came to dinner we can only surmise. The King most likely sat right opposite the salt cellar.

Exquisitely wrought silver salt cellars, sometimes eight or ten inches high, contained the precious seasoner, and as it passed from hand to hand it was handled with respect, for England's brine pits could supply but a fractional part of that nation's demand. Much had to be imported from the Continent.

There is a tradition, not entirely authenticated, that the city of London itself came into being as a byproduct, so to say, of the salt trade between the "tight little Island" and the Continent. An ancient route passed along where Westminster Abbey now stands on the banks of the Thames. Swelling the river out of its banks, spring and fall rains compelled the pack trains of salt (and doubtless other commodities) to wait until low water set in before crossing. A little settlement thus sprang up here to care for the freight—a sort of community warehouse; and that, so runs the tale, was the nucleus of London.

Even in early times salt making must have demanded special skills and techniques; for we know there was a Salters Guild of London composed of men who made and dealt in salt. Their trade mark showed three salt cellars on a shield spouting streams of salt from their sides.

Apparently the nobility wanted to keep salt scarce by keeping production down; and up to Queen Elizabeth's time each *wich* was allowed only twelve boiling days a year. Six in the spring, six in the fall. And at this point we find the two traditionally

belligerent Queens—Elizabeth of England, Mary of Scotland—
hard at it again. Mary started the ruckus.

The temperamental Scottish sovereign granted an inventive
Italian a patent to make salt near the Scottish border on condition that the heavy tax upon it should accrue to her treasury.
Enraged that her rival had thought of it first, Elizabeth decided
that she too would go into the salt making business. So off went
Lord Cecil, her emissary, to Jasper Seller, of Augsburg, Germany, with an invitation to come over and give her the low-down
on salt making. It is said that Elizabeth gave Seller a patent
in 1564.

He brought along fifteen iron pans forged in Germany. Competition began to run high between Scotland and England in
salt production. More salt was produced in both countries than
ever before. But the two Queens managed to keep prices high
because of the outlandish taxes. Resentment smouldered
throughout both countries.

"They tax our salt," swore many a stout yeoman. "Will they
next tax the very air we breathe?"

Salt producers shut down their plants. Smuggling and black
markets flourished, with whole villages conniving in the scheme.
A favorite trick was to smuggle cargoes of salt to Ireland and
run them back again to another and quieter port. For all that, the
tax remained for many years.

"Every year in England," wrote the Earl of Dundonald as late
as 1785, "ten thousand people are seized for salt smuggling and
three hundred men are sent to the gallows for contraband trade
in salt and tobacco." And the humane old nobleman goes on
to suggest remedies: tax the hearths in a home instead of the
salt which the family in that home uses. This measure of relief
he believed would place the burden of the duty upon the rich
instead of the poor. He also advanced the idea that rock salt
(discovered in England about 1670) be dissolved in seawater
and then the doubly strong brine evaporated.

In his campaign, Dundonald was assisted by the forthright

John Wesley, co-founder of Methodism, who directed the power of his fiery pen against the salt tax. But all this had no immediate effect upon the tax. Finally, from all over England rose a wail from the farmers that their hogs and cattle were dying from lack of salt. When, during Queen Anne's reign, the price of salt went to £30 sterling per ton, the people rose. Mobs, inflamed by hot-headed town meetings and blatant oratory, roamed across all England.

Englishmen of all ranks, the nobleman and the commoner joined in the protest. "A pig is a poor man's sinking fund," they said. "But the laws prevent a man from keeping a pig. What then shall he do?" At last, Parliament, frightened by the loud popular outcry, lowered the salt tax from fifteen shillings per bushel to two shillings. Then, after some months even this tax was removed and salt became a free commodity; and the good people of Merrie England were the merrier for it.

Meanwhile a new world had been discovered. . . .

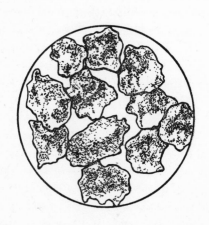

CHAPTER THREE

OLD WORLD—NEW WORLD

THE WORLD'S VARIOUS NATIONS have in the past made salt in various ways, the method depending on the source of supply, the quantity available and the facilities at hand. The Chinese, for instance, used a lotus seed for a salometer, and bamboo for almost every other utensil, including pipe. As in every such endeavor, success of production in the different countries and by the different means, has depended largely on the ingenuity and imagination of the several salt makers.

Nobody knows the age of the salt wells in China's Sze-chuan Province. They are of such antiquity that they have become "a part of things that are." At any rate, we do know they have been worked since 300 B. C. How they were discovered no one can say. But we know how they have been deepened from time to time through the centuries. Ancient writings tell of it.

First of all, the site for a well was selected by a geomancer— a chap who divined the spot by using figures and lines in an elaborate ceremony. After that, the well was sunk by the per-

Above illustration shows the "English Hour-Glass Master Salt Cellar," 15½ inches tall, 1492.

cussion method—i.e. repeated bangings with an iron drill on bamboo poles. A beam served as a lever, held up by a wooden frame. To operate, a half dozen men stepped on the long end of the beam; that raised the iron drill in the hole. Then, as one man, they all stepped off. Wham! The drill fell with great force. And woe to the man who was slow in stepping off! He was flung into the air like a child from the light end of a seesaw. And yet, astounding as it may seem, they could sink a well by this primitive method more than 3,000 feet deep—in from four to forty years.

"Self-flowing salt wells" exist in China similar to the natural brine springs of our own land. Nowadays the brine from other wells is brought to the surface by buckets attached by ropes or chains to steam winches—a sort of steam-operated, multiple-unit version of the Old Oaken Bucket. But long before steam, each well had a windlass with a clumsy, clattering wheel. A long bamboo tube brought up the brine, the tube being fastened by a rope to the windlass. Hard-driven water buffalo furnished the motive power. When they were lashed to a run, the bamboo tube came up filled with brine, which was emptied into kettles and evaporated by boiling over flames. Natural gas supplied fuel—gas from "fire-wells" (natural gas pockets) such as we have over here in the United States.

The Chinese in fairly recent years have developed modern methods, but the last World War drove them back to many of their primitive usages.

Dr. Pendleton, American soil scientist in Thailand during the war, tells how they make salt in that country. To each family is assigned its own section of the salt-springs region. They camp nearby and, during the sunny hours, some member of each family must stay on the job, splashing the brine about over the sun-heated rocks to induce quick evaporation. After a while, they scrape up the salt from the rocks and the sand, put it in baskets.

If you live in Australia, and are lucky, you may get your

salt from a "salt bush"—an actual shrub that has a high salt content.

In Japan, during the war, salt evaporating pans were heated by electricity; but because of the scarcity of "juice," the sun was called upon to help out on the Pacific beaches.

Java has some mud volcanoes which eject brine along with the mud; the natives gather and evaporate it.

Salt tablets, or coins, still circulate for money in some countries of Africa.

Salt is not so plentiful everywhere even today that men can use it to build houses. Yet Herodotus, Greek historian, in 425 B. C. tells of seeing salt houses near a salt mine in the Libyan desert.

"These people," he explained, "build their houses all of lumps of salt, since these parts of Libya are without rain."

Similarly, travelers in 1850 saw rock-salt houses in a section of the Sahara Desert, although other parts of the desert—notably near Bilma—have salt marshes where salt practically makes itself. Twice a week the native workers break up the salt crusts with sticks or by treading it down, wading waist deep in water. Thus it is more easily gathered, and a new crust may form.

Into the Mayo mines in India men and their families go with flickering lamps of vegetable oil, and knock out the rock salt. Swamp salt is plentiful in certain other parts of India; hundreds of tons of it are gathered annually and, since the government slaps a heavy tax on salt in most Indian provinces, the natives are continually getting into trouble for taking it out surreptitiously. Long ago, the rulers of India circumvented these salt thieves (if indeed men stealing an essential, such as salt, can be given that hard name) by driving herds of cattle into the swamp to destroy the supply by trampling it down so it would be no good to anybody. Dog-in-the-manger stuff!

In 1930, Mohandas Gandi, leading a protest march to the seashore, advised his Hindu followers to revert to the ancient custom of making sea salt rather than pay a salt tax to England.

In some places people get their salt by scraping it off the ground. There are dead lakes in Texas whose dried up bottoms used to supply salt to the Southern states. California also has dried up lakes. In many other places over the earth where the soil is salty, salt comes to the surface following rains and consequent evaporation. This "effloresced salt" as it is called, can often be observed on sand along the sea shore.

The great African explorer and missionary whom Henry M. Stanley greeted with "Dr. Livingston, I presume?" tells of seeing natives scrape effloresced salt from the ground; then they poured water over it, drained off the brine, boiled it down and shaped it into cones. In other sections salt mud was used as a basis for procuring the Seasoner. You will find the effloresced article still fairly common in India, Africa, Russia, and Argentina. The same Henry M. Stanley describes the gathering of salt at the Kapwe beds in India. Some Kapwe salt, he explains, comes from the natural hot salt springs of Kibiro; the natives evaporate the brine in open pans. Much more is reclaimed from Kapwe Lake into which the springs flow. Like the Dead Sea and our own Great Salt Lake, this body has no outlet. The floor is covered with a thick layer of deposited salt.

"You merely wade in and scoop up your salt," said Mr. Stanley.

In the Congo State, near the Congo River, there is a salt plain. The people fashion a funnel out of sticks, line it with large leaves. Into the funnel's bottom goes a filter of grass. Then they fill the funnel with salty earth; pour boiling water over it. The brine filters through into gourds or earthen jars. After which they mold the salt (obtained by boiling the brine) into cones— an impure product, but in great demand throughout this region.

Natives of Tunis get much of their salt from Shott-of-the-Palms, a small lake sixty feet below sea level. Here in summer a crust of salt forms so thick and hard that one may walk on it as on a frozen crust of snow. You can hear your footsteps echoing as when walking over a stone arch. Even caravans venture over it. The salt is cut and sawed like ice.

As told elsewhere, the old Romans depended upon sea salt. For storing, they piled it up in heaps and built fires close by. The salt piles turned black, but hardened under the heat and thus did not dissolve when it rained.

Apparently the Spaniards followed suit, for they showed the Indians this method of storing in their South American colonies.

Clarifying a Cloudy Subject

A clear brine makes a good salt. In certain parts of Europe the whites of eggs were added to boiling brine to clarify it. Blood from sheep or from black cattle (inexplicably) was used too, and sometimes even beer. These substances helped to form a scum which gathered some of the impurities as did egg shells which past generations of housewives put in the coffee pot. American salt makers early used many of these clarifying agents, not to mention tallow. Scientific methods do the trick today.

We know that the first American salt making by white men occurred along the Atlantic coast. The method: solar evaporation of sea water. In 1623 Robert Cushman, a member of the Plantation Company, wrote from England to Gov. Bradford of Massachusetts:

"We have now sent you, we hope, men and means to settle these three things: viz, fishing, salt-making and boat-making; if you can bring them to pass to some perfection, your wants may be supplied. The boat carpenter we sent is thought to be a fit man, the salt-man is skillful and industrious, and the preacher we have also sent is (we hope) an honest plain man, though none the most eminent and rare."

The carpenter turned out honest and industrious; the preacher we have no record of—but that salt-maker! Listen to Gov. Bradford's account of *him:*

"He whom they sent to make salt was an ignorante, foolish, self-willd fellow. He said he could do great matters in making salt works, so he was allowed to seek out fit ground for his purpose. After some search, he said he found a good place with a bottom that would hold salt water and which he doubted not would in a short time bring to all a great profit; but he must have ten men to be constantly employed. He was asked to be sure that the ground was good, otherwise he would bring a great charge by employing himself and so many men. But he was so confident that he caused them to send carpenters to rear a great frame for a large house to receive the salt. But in the end all proved vain. Then he laid the fault at the ground, in which he said he was deceived, saying if he could have lighter clay, he was sure then he could do it.

"Now it was seen that the whole attempt was a fraud. As he by his bold confidence and large promises deceived them in England that sent him, so he had wound himself into men's high esteem here. For he could not do anything but boyl salt in pans, and yet pretended there was so great a mystery in it as was not easy to be attained . . . .

"The next year he was sent to Cape Ann, and the pans were set up there where the fishing was. But before the summer was out, he burnt the house—which spoiled the pans, and this was the end of that chargeable business."

That was how they didn't make salt in Plymouth! A French nobleman named Blaise in *An Excellent Treatise of Fire and Salt* tells us how salt was being made in the Old World. Translated into English in 1649, in the dated spelling of his translator:

"There are two sorts of salt: Natural and Artificiall. The Natural growes in flakes, or in a rock by itself within the earth. The Artificiall is made with seawater or with liquor as a pickle drawn out of salty pits . . . which they boyle and congeal upon the fire."

Of the brine troughs, he explains: "You must courry this trough by Artifice that it drink not the water which men throw theron, which is done by beating it with a great number of Horses, Asses, and Mullets tied one with another that they may trample thereon so long that it be firm and solid as a certain barn floor."

Primitive Efforts in a New World

On a summer day in 1613 a group of exploring Englishmen from Her Majesty's Royal Colony of Jamestown, in "Virginea," lolled on the sandy beach of the fertile peninsula that divides Chesapeake Bay from the plunging Atlantic. Wistfully they looked across the sea toward the homeland they had left not many years ago. But there was no thought in their minds of returning. Here in America they had cast their lot, and here they would stay. But something angered them.

"Odds-bodkins!" exclaimed one of the group, "It gets my dander up the way these sea captains charge us for salt! There's Captain Christopher Newport and Captain Samuel Argall—fine seamen both, I grant ye. But they must slap enormous prices on the salt which they use for ballast in their boats and sell us when they bring in supplies. I tell you it's not to be borne! I paid out to Argall on his last trip five golden guineas for enough salt to last my family for a year!"

"I, too!" swore another, cynically. "But what—Heaven save us—is a man to do?"

"I' faith," broke in a third. "Listen to me. Over in England do they not make salt by letting the sun dry up seawater? We've seawater aplenty here. And feel the heat of yonder sun! I vow the sweat runs down my neck like a river."

No sooner suggested, than attempted. Those colonists built makeshift shallow wooden vats on the sandy beach near what became two and one-half centuries later the plantation of Governor Wise in Accomac County, Virginia. In these they imprisoned some seawater and let the sun evaporate it. The result was a coarse, sharp-tasting salt, unpalatable but usable. The news was hailed with jubilation in the Virginia colonies.

"No longer shall we have to depend upon England for salt!" they shouted.

This was one of America's earliest steps toward complete independence from the mother country. It occurred seven years before the Mayflower had touched upon the New England stern and rockbound coast. Moreover, it was the first attempt of Englishmen to make salt in what is now the United States. We hear much of Boston's tea party—that dramatic refusal of Massachusetts to receive England's favorite drink when taxed by England. But few people, I warrant you, have heard of Virginia's salt party—her own little private declaration of salt independence from Great Britain, written long ago in the saline waters of old Accomac.

English settlers brought their English customs and supplies with them to America. Then, finding that totally different conditions prevailed on these strange shores, they promptly set about developing new ways of doing things. This primitive effort at salt making is a case in point. What these Virginians did, however, was and for a long time continued to be, an individual chore in which one family (or sometimes a group of families) made salt from seawater for its own use in much the same way that it got its own soap from wood ash and grease, its own firewood and lumber from the forests, its clothing from family spinning wheels. It remained for thrifty New England to introduce commercial salt making. Up there, shrewd Samual Winslow, a man of stern and uncompromising stock, with a keen head for business on his shoulders, was the first of the commercial lads.

"I'm prepared to serve the good people of Salem with a continuing supply of most excellent salt," he announced in 1635.

Winslow built his salt plant on the Massachusetts seashore, applied for and received a patent—the first patent ever issued in America—to make as much salt as he could by his process. He made his profit but was not long without competitors. Little "salteries" sprang up at many points along the New England coast. It was pretty hard work. Two hundred and fifty to three hundred gallons of seawater equal seventy pounds of salt. Seventy pounds of salt equal one bushel.

Meanwhile down in New York State, we find a stout Dutch-

man, Dirck De Wolff, doing a rather good salt business with a
sun-evaporating plant at—you will never guess it!—Coney Island!
Could the good Dirck have looked ahead through the years and
envisaged the millions of surf bathers who one day would loll
about the area where he made salt (now a noisy national play-
ground) he would have blinked his blue eyes and in his stolid
Dutch way, exclaimed:

"Mij God! Wat zie en hoer ik!"*

Dirck also operated on a patent. But not from England.
He got his straight from the good burghers of Old Amsterdam
and it gave him the exclusive privilege to make salt for the
entire Royal Dutch Colony of New Amsterdam. Dirck's method
was to build shallow wood vats which he filled at high tide with
seawater. The sun, in time, evaporated the water, and there was
his salt. He found he had a ready sale for every bushel he could
gather. But down to Coney Island beach crowded other interested Dutch settlers.

"Get out!" they told Dirck. "Imposter! We want no manufacturing! We have our homes here!"

Undoubtedly this was the first instance of a restricted residential neighborhood in the new world—something people living in cities and suburbs were to hear much about in the years
to come. Testy old Governor Stuyvesant sent down an armed
guard to protect Dirck. But the irate citizens drove them off.

Wars have a way—as don't we all know from recent bitter
experience!—of skyrocketing the price of many an essential commodity. Salt came in for its share of inflation at the very beginning of our War for Independence. Here was a necessary article
and a scarce one, something which armies and civilians alike
had to have. The small American salt plants on the coast could
not supply this new national demand. Manufacture fell off when
the Colonies went to war. To make matters worse, the invading
Redcoats set about at once to find and destroy every salt pro-

---

* "My God! What do I see and hear!"

ducing plant they could lay their hands on. The price went to
$8.00 a bushel but people were glad to pay it—if they could get
the salt.

About half a century later, Napoleon Bonaparte bitterly observed that salt is a must in a soldier's diet. He should know! He'd
left 400,000 dead on the awful retreat from Moscow and attrib-
uted his men's inability to resist the hardship and cold of that
fearful ordeal to the lack of salt in their food.

The several states, in their saltless extremity, appointed com-
missions to study the situation and to find salt somewhere, some-
how, some way. Those appointed by New York were Mathew
Cantine, William Harper, and Major Jonathan Lawrence. They
made a preliminary survey of the state's manufacturing and natural resources; and upon their recommendation, the state
offered a prize of $500 each to the first five persons who would
set up plants and produce salt from seawater. The winners were
a group headed by the distinguished Revolutionary patriot,
Marinus Willett.

Willett and his associates built their shallow vats at Hunt-
ington, Long Island, and at Cold Spring, familiar North Shore
towns from which commuters every day travel to their daily
work in New York City. A windmill was used to pump seawater
into the vats to be evaporated by the sun. The venture started
with a flourish of great promise but came to an abrupt and tragic
end. The British won the Battle of Long Island and, with it,
the new salt works.

And then, in this desperate situation, someone in the assembly
remembered a little inland salt spring up on the lonely Indian
and owl-infested shores of Onondaga Lake. It was more than
350 miles northwest of New York City. To get there one had
to travel the Hudson and then the Mohawk in a canoe, and after
that long leagues of forest trails. One could, of course, go part
way by Oneida Lake.

"Get out there as quickly as you can," the Convention told
Peter Sims, "and see if you can get any salt from that spring.

You know about it. The French made salt there more than a century ago. Some say that Indians are still making it. We must have more salt—much more. It's worth the effort."

"I'll do my best," said Sims. And he did. But it wasn't enough in that wild and hostile region; the British and their Indian allies drove off Sims' party before he could get well started.

Other efforts in the East followed. At Islip, Sag Harbor, on the peninsula of Northaven facing Shelter Island, at various other points on Long Island, the desperate colonists made shift to get salt—get it by hook or crook. And history records that they did secure enough to get by.

Charles J. Werner, in his good little book with its long name, "A History and Description of the Manufacture and Mining of Salt in New York State," tells from the lips of an old resident an interesting incident connected with the Sag Harbor salt operation.

"The Sag Harbor whaling ships," so Werner recounts it, "used large quantities of salt foods on their long voyages. The necessity of providing a source of supply close to the port probably appealed to the pioneers in the whale fishery. So the whaling ships often anchored just off the salt works. The anchorage came to be called "Indian Jail" and goes by that name today for this reason: native Montauk and Shinnecock Indians (who, after landing from whaling voyages would get drunk and unruly) were confined in the ships' brigs at this point until they sobered up."

From such inconsequential incidents do historic nicknames derive and stick.

It is recorded, by the way, that there was once for a short time a salt plant on Manhattan Island. No one seems to know its exact location. It died in 1830.

During the Revolution the State of New Jersey also built and operated a series of evaporating plants along the coast— many of them at places since become famous as summer resorts. These helped, to a limited degree, the colonists' fight for salt.

Some excavations made in 1930 at the mouth of Oyster Cove on Forked River, near Barnegat, New Jersey, uncovered some large clay vessels well encrusted with salt. One was 15 feet in circumference. Arthur C. King, an authority on the Delaware Indians (who inhabited that region), explains that the red men made annual treks to the shore, after corn-planting time, to fish and make salt. Then they'd return home in the fall to harvest their crops, carrying back with them their sun-dried fish and the salt they had made in earthen pots.

Old residents of Barnegat claim to remember three Indian trails that once led from the interior to the shore at Barnegat.

They had good use for the salt, the red men. They employed it as white men use it today—they soaked their meat in brine and smoked it.

Salt making on Long Island remained a sizeable industry until near the middle of the Nineteenth Century. Somebody noted in 1849, however, that it was no longer a profitable enterprise. Salt by that time was coming from the interior to the coast, thus reversing the early movement by which it went inland from the coast settlements.

CHAPTER FOUR

BEYOND THE MOUNTAINS
LIES—*SALT*

PUT A COW TO GRAZE in a pasture where she must climb and descend a hill regularly, and in a very short time she will wear a path that follows inevitably the easiest possible grade between upland and base.

When the Indians crossed the Alleghany Mountains to the West that lay beyond, they took the trail which the buffalo, their predecessors, had worn for them because it was, literally, the line of least resistance. Next, white men with pack horses or in coaches or mountain wagons followed where the Indians went, for the identical reason.

Years went by. Came modern engineers, charting the course of railways and smooth-surfaced highways for motor vehicles. With their instruments, they merely confirmed, with a few straightenings of curves, the wild wisdom of the buffalo.

But the buffalo had not been the first. They were indeed comparatively recent visitors. One of these heavy-headed beasts was seen as late as 1815 in the western mountainous part of Virginia. There is ample evidence to show that some strange, ponderous, now extinct beasts had negotiated the same mountain passes aeons previously. They passed over the shaggy crests for the same reason that later the buffalo, the Indians, and—in large measure—the white men crossed. They were seeking salt, and salt "licks" or springs were known to be plentiful on the other side of the mountains.

"That country over yonder abounds with springs of common salt," said Thomas Jefferson, pointing west from the Albemarle slope where Monticello rested majestically on its hilltop. It was just at a time, very early in the Nineteenth Century, when men's thoughts were turning most longingly to the settlement of the vast valleys of the West. The Revolution was over. Independence had been won. The seaboard states were becoming crowded and everyone was talking "expansion." The new land beyond the mountains had been explored by pioneers sent out by President Jefferson and new settlers were rolling out to establish their homes there, where land was to be had for little more than the taking.

To the aging Jefferson, at his plantation home, they wrote and came for guidance.

"Is the land fertile?" they asked. "Are there running streams out there on which we can locate our homes? Where can we get our salt?"

And so Jefferson told them about the salt "licks"—places where for ages animals had come to lick the rocks and earth where the salt water bubbled up and where some of them left their bones. These same salt licks or springs would serve man also.

"Yes, there are plenty of places beyond the mountains, far from the seacoast, where settlers will find all the salt they need," Jefferson told them.

It had been an epochal event in the story of national settlement—finding salt in the wilderness. To the westward movement it imparted a mighty impetus.

The first white men to discover inland salt were certain of that hardy breed of French Canadian clerics who came down from the North bent upon the dual objective of Christianizing the redskins and establishing trade routes for Louis le Grand. Spearheading the procession was Pere Jerome L'Allemont. Down through northern New York he came, trudging with his guides, using his canoe where there was water, going on foot over the portages. He came to the shores of Onondaga Lake. Afterwards he wrote about his trip:

"A fountain from which very good salt is made by the Indians springs up in a beautiful plain surrounded by a fine wood. At eighty or a hundred paces from this salt spring, rises another of fresh water. These two take their birth from the bosom of the same hill."

Stand in the business center of modern Syracuse, New York, and look out along its busiest thoroughfare, while the motor cars whizz by you, and you can see the location of the salt spring which L'Allemont discovered less than thirty years after the English had made their first settlement at Jamestown. The thoroughfare appropriately is named Salina Street.

Following L'Allemont by seven years, came another exploring priest—Pere Simon Le Moyne—of distinguished family and name in American history. A kinsman, Bienville, founded the city of New Orleans; another, Iberville, settled Mobile. Pere Le Moyne accompanied a party of Huron and Onondaga chieftains to help them in writing a peace treaty between two of their belligerent tribes. He also found salt- and sweet-water springs, but Le Moyne did not stop with the mere discovery.

"We arrived at the inlet of a small lake (Lake Onondaga today) in a great basin half dry. We did taste the water of a salt spring nearby from which they (the Indians) dared not drink. There was a demon in it, they said, which rendered it fetid. Having tasted the water, I found it pure salt water. We made salt from it as natural as that from the sea." So runs Pere Le Moyne's record.

There you have the first known production of inland salt by white men within the borders of what is now the United

"A salt puddle surrounded by haystacks" — so early settlers described Saltville, Va., set among its shapely mountain peaks.

States. Long years would pass, however, before this spring would become important as a salt producer.

To the southward, meanwhile, the migrating fever spread inland from the coast toward the mountains even before the Revolution had made the colonies independent. From Jefferson's own Albemarle County on the Virginia slope, went forth Colonel James Patton, Commandant of Virginia Militia, to explore a corner of the state as far west as Kentucky. That was in 1747. In his party were Charles Campbell, Gent., and the Colony's surveyor, John Buchanan. Campbell found the upland airs of the Alleghanies delightful and there in the mountain wastes he had Buchanan lay out a tract of 350 acres along the shores of what he termed simply "Indian River." It is called the Holston now, and the tracks of the Norfolk & Western Railroad parallel it for many miles.

For this acreage Campbell obtained a royal patent from the Colonial Governor. It lay in a lovely cleft of the hills with pleasant peaks surrounding it; but more than one-third of his entire holding was covered by a marshy lake. That lake was briny—heavy with natural salt—a phenomenon here in the high 'Alleghanies where on all sides fresh water streams were born and coursed down to the valleys below. Campbell himself did not live to see his salt lake put to use.

Yet the time would come when the little town of Saltville, rising on the site of his mountain holdings, would produce annually a million bushels of salt—would for a time be the salt mainstay of one short-lived, ill-starred, and embattled nation, the Confederate States of America, which supplied its need for salt from this little highland settlement where the salt springs gushed forth so profusely that they formed a lake.

Not twenty miles away from Campbell's salt lake, two other of Colonel Patton's party laid out holdings and built themselves houses. Thomas Ingles and a kinsman, John Draper, chose a rolling domain on the mountain slope. They cleared out the forests and underbrush and called it Drapers Meadows. The beautiful grounds of the Virginia Polytechnic Institute in the town of Blacksburg are near the place where stood Ingles' great log house.

The lady of the Ingles household, young Mistress Mary Draper Ingles, then in her twenties, was walking in her flower garden on a warm Sunday afternoon in 1755. If anyone had told her that an army under General Braddock in Pennsylvania was even then being saved from complete annihilation at the hands of the French and Indians by another young Virginian named George Washington, she would not have believed it.

Mary's husband, Thomas Ingles, had ridden off to a distant field, then nearly ready for harvesting. Her father was away on some errand connected with the local parish. Inside the big log house, Colonel Patton, the Commandant, was guest of the house and sitting before the writing desk making out his report to Richmond on the supplies of powder and ball which he was distributing to the frontier settlements. That was how he happened, that day of all others, to be at Thomas Ingles' home. There were rumors, moreover, that hostile Indian bands were coming east from the Ohio country.

Now the story of Mary Ingles is intimately connected with the story of early American salt making. Mary carried her first child in her arms. Had you seen her, walking about among her rose bushes, culling a bloom here and there, doubtless singing a happy little song, you would have known at once that another child was on the way.

What was Mary Ingles like? I have seen the portrait of a strong-faced, wrinkled old lady which was said to be Mary, in the white winter of her age. Her great grandson, Dr. Hale, has written that she was a tomboy in her young maidenhood. Anyhow, I like to think of her as being tall, fine looking, well put-up and lovely, with enough feminine daintiness to make her enjoy her flower garden on the outpost. I like to think of her as possessing also a heavy vein of iron running the length of her shapely back; a reserve of fortitude which enabled her to undergo torturing experiences, to come out of them smiling, and leave to posterity an epic of frontier heroism.

It was getting on toward sunset there in Mary Ingles' garden. She heard a slight stirring in the thick underbrush that enclosed the planted flower space. Then, before she knew what was happening a party of painted Shawnee Indians had leaped into the open, seized and gagged her, and slipped off with her and the baby into the woods. Mary had time only to let out one yell. No one heard it but Colonel Patton, making out his report there in the house. He seized his pistols and sabre and rushed out to catch a glimpse of the marauders disappearing with their captives through the forest.

The Colonel was a seasoned Indian fighter. He let go with

both pistols, got an arrow in his shoulder, and shouted for aid. By the time a pursuit posse could be organized in that isolated vicinity, the attackers (more than thirty of them, it was later discovered) were well out over the hills and heading straight through the gap toward the headwaters of New River.

Reading the record, one cannot help wondering why the Indians did not kill Mary Ingles and have done with it. A young and comely woman among savages, if held alive, would be held, one would naturally suppose, but for one purpose. Yet there is not the slightest evidence that I have been able to discover that Mary Ingles was ravished. Her great grandson, John Hale, who wrote of her adventures, advances the theory that her captors were holding Mary for ransom. If so, why did they take her four hundred miles west to Ohio and Kentucky without demanding the cash or its equivalent?

That girl must have had in her veins blood which flowed in the men of Hastings, Agincourt, Marston Moor, and Culloden; of ancestors who had endured imprisonment, torture, and hardship; holding to life as a sacred trust when it would have been so much easier to have given it up.

The savages dragged Mary along with them. She found that the attack on her home was but an incident in a county-wide foray—one of a whole series of attacks in which massacre, burning and theft were involved. To her joy, or to her sorrow, she discovered among the few other captives her own sister-in-law, Betty Draper. The two women lent strength to one another. Mary needed in the worst way a woman's assistance just then.

Once Mary stumbled and her child fell from her arms. A brave stooped, picked it up and returned it to her. Now began the long hard trek westward through the hills. A night or two out, the party stopped at a quiet place and there Mary had her new baby. Then they moved on again, and for a considerable distance Mary was permitted to ride one of the stolen horses. Through the river gorges they went, out on the levels where New River, joining with another stream from the north, makes

the smooth Kanawha. After that the going was less strenuous.
For several days they went on down the widening valley, stopping finally at a buffalo lick. It was six miles from where, a century later, the city of Charleston, West Virginia's capital, would stand.

Here the party rested for many days while the Indians put Mary and Betty to work making salt. This was something none of the white people had seen before. Up to that time all Virginia had been depending for salt upon the Virginia coast solar plants and salt importations. Mary seems to have caught on quickly. The redmen kept her and Betty busy over the kettles for weeks. Strange—that the spot on which they worked would become America's second most important early salt-producing center, and Mary's great grandson would one day head a mighty salt trust established on this very spot.

Dipping the brine from the shallow spring, boiling it over a fire in a pot swung on poles, watching the water gradually vanish and leave the dirty white lumps in the kettle's bottom; then scraping out that residue, while still damp, and packing it into blankets and deerskin sacks to take along with them—that was the way the time passed for Mary Ingles and Betty Draper.

At last the party moved on. They left the buffalo lick, went on down the Kanawha Valley to the Ohio, followed that river to a point fifty miles below the present site of Cincinnati. There they crossed the river and went on to Big Bone Lick, another salt spring which was to attain some importance in later years. Here Mary and Betty once more were put to work at the salt kettles.

It was here that the two Virginia women, together with several German women captured in the Shenandoah Valley, formulated a plan of escape. Apparently it was this: whoever had the first opportunity would slip away from the camp, make her way back to Drapers Meadows and send back a rescuing party. Meanwhile Mary's older child had been killed. An Indian, angered at its continual wailing, beat its brains out against a tree. We are not told how Mary survived the shock, only that she did.

The first chance of escape came to Mary. That meant leaving her second baby, a fearful choice. Perhaps she placed the larger duty—trying to get help for the other captives—above her filial love. In any case, escape she did, unarmed. She made her tortuous way on foot back through the valleys of Kanawha and New Rivers and, after forty days, reached Drapers Meadows. She had nothing to eat on the way but roots and berries, and such other wild fruit as she could find.

She roused the countryside and it is recorded that Mrs. Betty Draper and the baby were rescued.

Mary Draper Ingles had thus made salt at two important licks in the West—Kanawha and Big Bone. Her knowledge of salt making, learned from the Indians, she brought back to Drapers Meadows, and it was not long before salt was being made at the spring which bordered Campbell's lake—the beginnings of Saltville.

Battles have raged around salt.

CHAPTER FIVE

BY THE DARK SHORES OF ONONDAGA

"THAT LITTLE SALT SPRING at Onondaga." So the coast dwellers of New York City and New England spoke of it — rather slightingly. They heard about this spring from returning travelers. They'd read of it in historical and contemporary accounts. For more than a century, they knew, sojourning Frenchmen had made salt up there. More, too, the French had taught the Indians to overcome their superstition about "that demon in the water." So that now, from town to town in upstate New York as far east as Albany, the redskins periodically appeared and peddled their damp, dirty-looking but still potent product from the self-same spring. "Indian salt" was bought and used freely.

To whom did the spring now belong? Old Sir William Johnson

in Colonial days had persuaded the Indians to deed him all the land encircling the lake, which included, of course, the salt spring. Men living in New York City still remembered that incident and laughed at it. Some had been present at the ceremony and told of it with great relish—Sir William, sitting there majestically in the open grove under the trees, lining up every man-jack of the tribe and his squaw to boot, and making each and every one sign with his or her mark the deed of transfer! The first time, surely, the rights of women were recognized in the New World! Sir William was taking no chances.

But that was long ago. Sir William was dead and the British power forever broken in the American colonies. Therefore, who now owned the salt spring of Onondaga? Would the title revert to the Indians? That question faced the New York Assembly.

According to hearsay, there wasn't very much to lay claim to: only a salty mudhole in sinister, remote Onondaga. Chase, the historian, speaks of the area as being "deep, noisome, miasmatic." It was mucky with the upsurgings of earth water no less than the rain-water swamps that overlaid the wide bottoms a large part of the year. Dark and forbidding forests hemmed it in— jungles in which wild animals lived in great numbers so as to be close to the salt, joining their yowlings with the lamentations of countless owls, making the night hideous.

In the very midst of the worst section of this desolation was known to be the spring which yielded natural brine, a few hundred feet away from the lake shore. But no available white man knew its exact location. Some said the spring was on the east side of Onondaga Creek. Some said that it lay to the west of the creek.

The year 1787 swept across America when the Nation's new Constitution was on every statesman's tongue. In that year one man had the hardihood to make his home in the Onondaga region. He was Ephraim Webster, trapper, who built his cabin near the lake and hunted and traded with the savages. The year following, however, a newcomer moved in; Colonel Asa Danforth and his family from Worcester, Mass. They arrived in a heavy wagon and put up a house of their own.

"Whut in the name of heaven, stranger, ever made you come out to these here God-forsaken parts?" Eph asked.

If Danforth answered truly, he replied that he was dead broke and had to seek a livelihood. Also, he had some ideas about making salt at the spring. That is, if he could find the infernal thing in the maze of forests, swamp, and brush that cluttered the lake shore.

"You won't get no redskin to tell you where that spring is at," Webster most likely told him; but Danforth was not easily discouraged.

Danforth was a sturdy man—elderly, upright, and dependable. He had come out of the Revolution a brigadier general, though people still called him "Major." He'd fought at Lexington with the embattled farmers. Then General Israel Putman had induced him to sign up with the Regulars. From then on, Danforth's rise was rapid, as one of Putman's dependable lieutenants.

He went into the fight a wealthy man, proprietor of a flourishing little forge and foundry in Worcester that would have made him independent for the rest of his life. He came out of the war penniless; for, patriotically, he had turned over his plant to the Government, upon request. The Government paid him off in Continental currency, worth nothing. And so, he told Webster, here he was on the ragged fringe of nowhere to look into this matter of salt.

Fortunately, Danforth was joined that same year by another and younger settler from the East—Comfort Tyler of Connecticut. He came also to hunt for salt. Tyler was a surveyor who had tramped the woods since boyhood. He knew the Indians, and they liked him. When only thirteen, he had seen actual service in the Revolution, and was made a Colonel when barely of age. Now he watched the spread of America inland from the coast.

"They're going to need salt out there in the West," he said

The names of these two loom large in America's salt history.
Tyler and Danforth—first white American salt makers at
Onondaga.

They put their heads together and made their plans.

"The first thing to do," Danforth said, "is to find that salt
spring. How are we going to do it?"

"I'll find out from the Indians, sir. I understand them. They'll
tell me."

"Well, good luck to you, Colonel! If you can make those red
rascals show you where that spring is, the whole state will owe
you a debt of gratitude."

It was early May of 1788. With his servant, Tyler left home
at daylight. He lugged a fifteen gallon kettle to their canoe and
paddled out along the shore some distance. Before long, an
Indian hailed them. By signs and by the use of the few words
he knew of their language, Tyler asked to be shown the salt
spring, motioning to the kettle. What persuasions or blandish-
ments he used are not of record. But they were successful. Here
is his own account of it:

"I went with this Indian guide and we steered out the mouth
of Onondaga Creek easterly, into a pass since called Mud Creek.
After passing over the marsh, then flowed by about three feet
of water, and steering towards a bluff of hard land, the Indian
at last fastened the canoe and pointed to a hole in the ground
a short distance from the lake's brink. It was filled with water.

" 'Ugh!' he said. 'Salt!' "

Tyler reported that he worked well into the late afternoon
and made fifteen bushels of salt.

It is pleasant to picture him—this eager young forerunner
of America's industrial era—as he and his servant labored there
on the edge of a muddy spring which the Indians had enlarged
by digging around it. A spring which was to be the fountain
head, in very truth, from which a vast industry was to flow.

Dipping out the brine, filling their kettle, and boiling it over
a wood fire, he watched eagerly as the water bubbled and surged

and finally dwindled away, leaving on the kettle bottom the grainy mass for which there was a rising national demand.

On his next salt-making expedition, Tyler took Danforth with him. From a contemporary account, we gather an excellent idea of the caliber of that rugged patriot. Much of this ten-mile journey, says the record, was made on foot and the old Major, using his coat as a cushion, carried the kettle on his head the entire distance without once putting it down to rest.

They swung it on a cross pole supported by two crotched sticks and within a day or two made enough salt to last their respective families for months. The efforts of these two pioneer white salt makers thus far, mark you, were merely to supply their personal needs. In a short time both would become important salt manufacturers in an industrial community. They started the ball rolling.

As a result of Tyler's and Danforth's efforts, the State of New York obtained from the Indians a mile-wide girdle of land surrounding the lake which was known to contain the salt spring. Later that girdle was much enlarged. To the Indians they gave the right to make as much salt as they needed for their own supply.

Yet neither to Danforth nor Tyler goes the credit of making the first *commercial* inland salt by a white man. That honor belongs to Nathaniel Loomis. Loomis and his party came paddling a small flotilla of canoes from Lake Oneida, through Oneida River and connecting water courses, to Onondaga. Loomis had large ideas. He brought fifteen kettles and in a few days had a well going.

"I worked all through the fall and winter," Loomis reported, "and by spring had five hundred bushels of salt."

This he took back to the little settlements in and around Oneida and sold it at $1.00 per bushel.

Commercial inland salt thus was sold by white men for the first time in 1790. At that very time, down in the Kanawha Valley of Virginia (as is told in detail in another chapter) other pioneers were busy making salt from the rich brine licks of that region. But it was not until seven years after Loomis had made and sold his first supply of the Onondaga product that Elisha Brooks, in Kanawha, built his first salt furnace, forerunner of the great salt development of that valley.

This old salt kettle at Grand Saline, Texas, memorializes the State's earlier salt industry.

CHAPTER SIX

SALINA GETS GOING

WILLIAM VAN VLECK and Jeremiah Gould came shortly after Loomis, and with them came another advance in technique. They dug a well a few feet deep near the lake shore. Then, instead of swinging their kettles from horizontal poles or from tripods, as the Indians did, they held them stationary by fastening them solidly in stone foundations, secured by mortar mixed with mud. They left space underneath for the fires. In this way, the pot did not swing from side to side and was more easily stirred. These two experimenters used larger-size cauldron-type kettles, in shape resembling a half orange with the meat removed, with round bottoms. Their four kettles bubbled merrily away and they ladled out the salt when the water was gone. It was a big step in the right direction, though in order to carry enough water from the spring by hand, to keep those big kettles going, they had to hustle like boys carrying water for the elephants on circus day.

Three years later, Moses DeWitt joined Van Vleck, bringing with him yet another improvement. He built an open wood trough from the spring (which was up the slope and a little way from the lake shore) to the kettles. This let the brine flow by gravity in a steady stream which could easily be blocked off at the source as occasion required. Adding some little side spouts. leading from the main trough into each kettle, gave DeWitt a crude, but perfectly workable system of feeding the brine.

From the rounded, inverted appearance of his four stone kettle bases, DeWitt called his little plant "salt arches". The name clung. For years to come, people would speak of the numerous salt operations at Onondaga as "arches"—a term peculiar to that region. Later they came to be known as salt blocks. In Kanawha and at Pomeroy, Ohio, as well as at some other salt-making centers, the plants were simply "furnaces."

Try to picture that primitive salt operation at Onondaga— four thirty-five gallon stationary kettles boiling away in the wilds of upstate New York and a continuous flow of natural brine feeding steadily from spring to kettle. It is important in history. For that method, though with numerous improvements through the years, was the system employed for the next three-quarters of a century in most parts of the United States.

It is difficult for us, to whom salt is today so commonplace and accepted an article that we never think of the possibility of not having it, to comprehend the significance of this first forward step in its manufacture: a continuous process of production. It so increased the output that before many months Onondaga salt makers were supplying the whole county and reaching out to adjacent counties, where many settlers were now building their homes and incorporating villages. The next step followed naturally; reservoirs to store up brine from the spring, thus maintaining a constant supply.

There seems to have been room enough for every salt prospector. Experimenters soon found that one had but to dig down a few feet at almost any place not far from Onondaga's shore to strike brine. Better still, the deeper you went, the stronger the brine became. And so well-digging boomed.

The State of New York, you recall, had got the salt lands from the Indians. It now assumed a coordinating control over salt production, leasing the salt-making rights to any legitimate applicant for a nominal consideration. The requirements were modest. If you desire to make salt, said the State, go ahead and make it; dig your well, set up your arches, and get going. You must make at least ten bushels per kettle per year. Pay the State four cents per bushel for each bushel you make, sell your output at not more than sixty cents per bushel, and you will realize a reasonable profit.

Thus did New York's early "OPA" work, and it seems to have gone along very well indeed, if one may judge by the rapid growth of the salt industry.

The State's salt lands included 15,000 acres, none of which could be used as military grant land to soldiers who fought in the War for Independence.

"Sign away New York's valuable salt properties?" declared the State legislature. "Never!"

"More salt land than the State will ever need!" scoffed the objecting minority, who were sadly mistaken. So great was the rush of salt makers to the new settlement around the springs (now a bustling town called Salina) that before 1822, the acreage had all been preempted and many wells were being sunk on contiguous private property.

Here is the way the State operated. It appointed a superintendent and paid him a good salary—$850 a year. William Stevens was the first to hold office. The State put up a warehouse, located in the center of what is now Syracuse's Clinton Square. The superintendent assigned to each approved applicant a plot of land on which to set up his plant. It was up to him to clean off the timber and burn the sedge. Leases were for three years with option of renewal.

As the salt came from kettles it was dried and packed into barrels. The barrels were sent by ox-drawn wagons to the State warehouse. There the brand or mark of the manufacturer was clearly stamped on each container. The individual salt makers then took orders for the salt and turned them over to the superintendent, who released the proper number of barrels from the respective makers' stock. Also, it was the custom from time to time for the superintendent to do a little selling on his own account from the stock of the various makers on hand. And one can only surmise that the State superintendents were extremely honest men. Otherwise, think of the enormous possibilities for favoritism and graft which were open to them!

In addition to the four-cent tax paid to the State, an additional one cent per bushel was paid for storage at the warehouse.

Now began a period of expansion at Onondaga that testified to two things—America's enormous need for salt as it then prevailed, and the eagerness of settlers in western New York to get going industrially.

The first year of operation at Salina saw several arches going. The warehouse handled 25,000 bushels that year; and whereas the trade had been local at the start, it now began to cover a wide territory, reaching eastward to Albany and down the river towards New York City.

The second year's output was 56,000 bushels. The year 1801 rolled up a total of 62,000 and so well had the salt warehouse become known that its certificates apparently were recognized as virtually legal tender.

"The superintendent," writes the historian Werner, "sometimes issued certificates for salt deposited and these were bought and sold, giving the storehouse some of the characteristics of a bank."

The largest firm of early salt makers at Salina was called simply The Federal Company. It comprised a group of most honorable men—if one may judge by the Old Testament quality of their given names. There were Asa Danforth, the granddaddy of them all; Elisha Alvord, and Jedediah Sanger. Also there was

Daniel Keeler and Ebeneezer Butler and Hezekiah Olcott. Finally there was Thomas Hart. This group put up the largest manufacturing building in town. It contained thirty kettles set in arches and was the wonder of the people—the first hint of the big building development of the city of Syracuse. But new wells were constantly being dug and within a year a still bigger building with forty kettles arose.

Some of the desolate and overgrown appearance which marked the Onondaga region was now retreating before the growth of this little salt settlement. Dr. Benjamin DeWitt, secretary of the Society for the Promotion of Agriculture, Arts, and Manufacturers, visited Salina in 1801. The village, according to the good Doctor, stood upon a little upland thirty or forty feet above the lake level. Close by lay a marshy stretch in which were the salt springs or wells. All about rose the dark forests, though the cleared area was now large enough to present a cheerful and busy appearance. The buildings were from twenty to thirty feet wide and of varying lengths, depending upon how many kettles that particular salt maker had going.

"The furnaces," wrote Dr. DeWitt, "are placed along the side of the building with their mouths opening into it. The other side is generally made use of to pile salt for the purpose of draining off the brine and allowing it to dry, immediately after it comes from the evaporating vessels. The furnaces are built of stone. Two or three kettles (such as are used to boil potash, containing each about 80 gallons) are usually placed over each furnace. Between each two furnaces a large trough is placed. From this the water is drawn into the boilers [he means kettles] as often as is required. These troughs are continually kept filled with brine by means of gutters into which it is pumped out of the springs. The furnaces being supplied with fuel, and the kettles filled with brine, they are allowed to boil briskly. After a while the 'powder scratch,'* as it is called, begins to precipitate on the bottom. This is removed as fast as it forms. . . ."

---

*i.e. A mixture of various bitter compounds.

The Doctor explained that the removal of this refuse (commonly spoken of in the salt industry as "bittern") was accomplished by the use of "bittern pans." These were nothing but shallow vessels like giant pie pans, each with a long wooden handle which extended above the surface of the boiling brine and by which the salt boiler could lift the bittern pan out as occasion required. Even with the use of bittern pans, however, a salt kettle could not be used longer than about ten days steadily. Then it had to be cooled off and the accumulated "powder scratch" chipped off.

"Next," Dr. DeWitt continues, "the salt begins to crystallize; the kettles are then suffered to boil gently till nearly all the water is dissipated. The salt is then taken out (by ladles) and deposited in proper places to drain off the water and suffer it to dry. Nothing now remains in the kettle but a small quantity of "bittern." This is thrown away and the process begins all over again . . . . Thus simple is the whole process which is used in manufacturing a beautiful white granulated (! !) salt from the waters of these valuable springs."

DeWitt wrote that in 1801. There were then 157 kettles going and each of the big ones yielded one bushel and one peck of salt for each boiling. There were smaller sized kettles too. The total output of that year, said the writer, was expected to be 70,000 bushels. Actually it was 62,000.

You notice DeWitt mentions the salt water being pumped to the arches. Following the first effort to make it flow by gravity— a frequently impossible objective, due to the respective locations of spring and plant—a crude hand pump had been constructed, by which human muscle increased the flow of brine to supply all the plants.

And well digging went on. James Geddes, a name to be reckoned with in these parts when we come to the all-important factor of transporting salt, sank a well and set up his arches at a little settlement several miles up the lake shore. The town of Geddes is there yet. For years it was a great producer of salt, and its chief manufacturer was Geddes himself. You will read more of him as we go along.

John Danforth, brother of Asa, started another plant at a small town, which he named Liverpool, at the far north end of the lake. Thus by the turn of the century, says Werner, "there was a complete string of salt works around the lake, starting at Liverpool on the north, including Salina and ending at Geddes on the southwestern shore."

Parenthetically, the FTC today would frown upon the name "Liverpool." The town was very likely named so its product could be called "Liverpool Salt." Buyers would thus think it came from Liverpool, England.

Years later, in Kansas, there was a way station near Hutchinson named "Saginaw," and some early racketeers sold "Saginaw Salt" from Kansas! (See later chapters on Kansas and Michigan salt making.)

Meanwhile the salt makers who built their little homes at Liverpool built a school also, and sent their boys to it.

"Our trouble is this," complained Master Conker, the pedagogue, "the school is so close to the salt works that I find my scholars paying more attention to the progress of salt making than studying the three R's and making their pothooks and handles."

This boys' school ran for ten years and constantly enlarged its curriculum. For a part of that time it was located directly in one of the old salt blocks and so close to the furnaces that the school, in winter, was heated from it. In summer—no record is given as to how the pupils kept cool.

Later, apparently, the Liverpool salt men took a great interest in this school and contributed jointly to its support. Its courses included history, bookkeeping, business arithmetic and similar subjects designed to fit the young hopefuls for positions in the companies' offices. If there is an older business college in the United States, I have not heard of it.

Social events for young and growing communities—Salina,

Syracuse, Liverpool, Geddes—sometimes centered about the salt blocks. It was fun for the young folks to have picnics there. They would cook potatoes, roast sweet corn within the shuck, and broil fresh steaks on the still-hot stones. Frying-size chickens would broil nicely over the coals and a good time would be had by all. At least, so remembers one of Syracuse's elderly ladies whose memory, unclouded and alert, retains it from her father's telling.

Asa Danforth, pioneer salt man, had a son, Asa Junior, who in 1805 introduced horsepower for brine pumping, replacing the manpower hitherto used. And that wasn't all. Horsepower, in turn, gave way to waterpower, for Asa next conducted the water of Yellow Brook in a mill race from the new little settlement of Syracuse, or South Salina, to Salina—a distance of not many rods. This water ran a wheel which turned the pump, which elevated the brine, which made the salt which seasoned and preserved the food of dwellers of New York State. In this connection we have the first reference to Syracuse—a small growth of little houses and arches just to the south of the larger Salina, which in time would, municipally speaking, be gobbled up by the newcomer.

Photo Bettmann Archive

They used girls to pack salt at Syracuse in 1870.

The senior Danforth, a member of the big Federal organization, appears no more in the salt making annals of Onondaga, though it is certain that he retained his interest in the business. Indeed, he was for a short time the State superintendent. Later he became judge of the Common Pleas Court, State Senator at Albany, a Major General of New York Militia.

As for Comfort Tyler, his associate. Tyler remained for years an active salt maker at Salina-Syracuse, meanwhile plying his profession of surveyor. He helped settle the New York-Pennsylvania State boundary line and several other interstate disputes. The Indians loved him and trusted him as no other man since Sir William Johnson. They called him To-Whon-Ta-Qua: "double man—both laborer and gentleman." He went briefly to the State Assembly at Albany. But Tyler's middle years were blackened by his association with Aaron Burr's treasonable expedition against New Orleans.

It is recorded that Tyler, in aid of Burr's enterprise, had slaughtered and salted down more than 1,000 hogs. These he loaded on barges on Beaver Creek in Pennsylvania and floated into the Ohio and to the island home of Harmon Blennerhasset, where Burr was busy hatching his schemes. A welcome addition to Burr's store of provisions were these barges and their valuable cargoes. Tyler later went on down the Ohio and Mississippi with his four barge loads to connect with Burr at Natchez who had preceded him there. But at Natchez he, along with a number of other "conspirators," was taken into custody.

Indictments for treason, lodged against Tyler and his associates, however, seem never to have been brought to court. Tyler returned to New York State, lived down the scandal, and died a respected and beloved citizen, retaining to the end his interest in salt making.

He was the first man to transport salted pork on the Ohio River, a stream which was later to bear millions of tons of it, in the days when Cincinnati would be the meat-packing center of the world, rejoicing in the nickname "Porkopolis."

CHAPTER SEVEN

THIS IS THE DITCH
THAT SALT BUILT

BOOM! RESIDENTS OF SALINA and Syracuse awoke one morning in October, 1825, to the sound of cannon firing, and knew what it meant. The Erie Canal was open — clear through from Buffalo on Lake Erie to Troy on the Hudson River; the waters of the Atlantic thus legitimately wed to those of the Great Lakes The idea of using cannon to announce the event was Governor DeWitt Clinton's. He'd strung field guns all the way from Buffalo to Troy within "hearing distance," spaced so that the firing of the first communicated the news to the second, the second to the third, and so on. A sort of pre-Morse telegraph by which to notify the people within the short space of an hour or two that the East and the West had been joined by a canal—built by salt.

They dug it in sections—this big ditch for which Clinton and many others had labored so long. Several months earlier the people of Syracuse and Salina had celebrated the coming of one of those sections to their doors and the memory of that gala event was yet fresh in their minds. Especially they were thrilled by Governor Clinton and his entourage, guests at their board, making oratory such as they had never heard before.

And James Geddes had spoken, too; Geddes who had brought the route of the canal cutting through their very midst; who had laid out the new and growing section of South Salina on two hundred and fifty acres. That was the town now called Syracuse, incorporated as a village in 1812, fourteen years after Salina; and before a year had passed Syracuse had a general store, within two years more a library and a jail, and was otherwise marching right along.

They remembered the first boat coming up the canal. She was the *Montezuma,* drawn by four high-stepping, strapping draft horses and followed by a strung-out fleet of packets, freight boats, and indiscriminate craft, all gay with bunting. Too, there was a floating Noah's Ark and circus, displaying bears, eagles, reptiles, and highly painted Indian chieftains The liquor flowed and the barbecued beef was seasoned with Onondaga salt from their own blocks

And now the whole job was done, as announced by the cannon! The Erie Canal, longest in the world, was open for business from end to end. Onondagans went back to making salt again, James Geddes among them.

Like Comfort Tyler, James Geddes knew how to get along with the Indians, and he seems to have gotten along with everyone else, too. The Onondagas adopted him into their tribe and gave him the name that sounds a lot like that of the lake by whose shores he founded the small salt town still known as Geddes: they called him Don-Da-Dag-Wa. The white residents of the entire region soon recognized his worth.

A keen, self-taught farmer from Carlisle, Pennsylvania, Geddes possessed a mighty hunger for book learning. He said that as a boy following the plow, he would ease up at the end of a long furrow, wind the lines around the plow handles and let the team rest while he read from a book continually carried in his pocket. Thus in time he got the rudiments of his education as a surveyor and engineer.

It was early in the nineteenth century when he visited Salina for the first time, and for the same reason that everyone else came: salt. Standing upon a little rise of ground, he looked down over the sprawling, bustling new community with its straggling huts. The wood smoke from its furnaces was sharp in his nostrils. Slightly to the south of the town and a few rods distant he could see that other sprouting village with its few wells and homes—South Salina, now coming to be known as Syracuse. It was a fairly level location but, one would say, an extremely unhealthy place to live. It looked as though malaria stalked through it yearly, taking a toll. He could see the state's salt works superintendent making his tour of inspection, going from plant to plant in a rowboat. That was healthier than wading, and that was why all the houses were built on stilts. Geddes also saw the men swarming about the plants—rough, bearded fellows in coonskin caps and leather breeches.

What he saw, however, satisfied him. He went back to Pennsylvania, lined up a number of other men with capital and returned with the equipment to start his plant. Now Geddes was not just another salt maker. He seems to have been the first of the lot to grasp the essential interrelation of salt and transportation. His public spirited interest in his new home town shortly made him a justice of the peace and to the day of his death he was called Judge Geddes.

"If the salt industry is to expand," Geddes told his townsmen, "we must reach the big markets, both east and west of us. What we need is a deep, dependable channel and big boats for steady shipment."

His ideas were exactly in line with those of many prominent

New Yorkers of that day, such men as DeWitt Clinton, Robert Fulton, Robert Livingston, Killean Van Renssalaer, and others. They were busy promoting a canal to connect the Great Lakes and the Atlantic Ocean. Various routes were proposed, many of which entirely bypassed Salina and Syracuse.

The original canal promoters had one long-range objective which was this: Divert the trade of the new West (the Ohio and Mississippi Valleys) eastward to the port of New York. It was now moving down the western rivers in barges and flatboats and some new-fangled paddlewheelers to New Orleans. Thence it went by sailing ships, up the coast to the big eastern cities and to foreign ports.

"That's all very well," says Geddes impatiently to the assembled residents of Salina-Syracuse. "But what we need right now is a canal to move our salt to market."

So, with that in view, Geddes gets himself appointed engineer of the proposed canal. His instructions from the Canal Commissioners are "to study and examine what may be the best route of the proposed canal." He does a thorough job of it. Disregarding all other suggested routes, he lays out the canal direct from Troy to Buffalo, using in part the channel of the Genesee and Mohawk Rivers, and straight through the heart of Salina.

Some salt men objected. "That's going to mean higher taxes."

"You can afford to pay them," Geddes answered quietly. "You will sell more salt than you ever dreamed of making."

And in the ensuing canal agitation the potential volume of salt which the new waterway would carry was used as an argument in its behalf.

Geddes' prophetic words were more than fulfilled. Without the 12½ percent tax which the state at once slapped upon the salt makers, the canal could not have been built. That tax and subsequent tolls on salt cargoes paid for nearly half the entire cost of building the canal. During the almost century-long life of the Erie Canal as an important highway of transportation, salt remained its best customer.

If you travelled via the New York Central Railroad across New York State, any time in the early years of the present century you could have seen from your car window one of the remaining snub-nosed canal boats moving, salt-laden, along the canal's placid channel; the sturdy team trotting along the towpath up ahead; the driver, most likely, astride one of his beasts; his wife on deck at the tiller, and the friendly smoke issuing from the little kitchen at one end of the pot-bellied craft.

Carrying salt on the Erie Canal fostered a breed of two-fisted, hard-drinking, free-living boatmen, who prided themselves on their toughness. It must have been worth a long journey just to see the canal boats moving out of Syracuse in a trailing procession, stubby prows sending the water on either side in long ripples, the horses snorting clouds of steam in the fresh morning air, the boatmen shouting a song that went something like this:

> We're loaded down with sin and salt,
> We're plumb chock full of rye.
> And the Captain he looks down at me
> With his mean and wicked eye.
>
> Oh, the E-r-i-e is rising,
> The strap is hangin' low,
> And I swear I think
> We'll git no drink
> Till we get to Buffalo.*

And then, arriving at the canal terminal in Buffalo, the salt boatmen, after delivering their cargoes, would go strutting through the streets, seeking excitement to the old familiar tune:

> Buffalo Gals, won't you come out tonight,
> Won't you come out tonight, won't you come out tonight,
> Buffalo Gals, won't you come out tonight
> And dance by the light of the moon.*

Yes, moving salt and other cargo on the Erie Canal was an interesting and profitable business. A boatman had to work hard, driving his team and getting in his cargo. But there was a fascination in moving from town to town—Albany, Canajoharie, Schenectady, Yuttica (Utica), Rome, Syracuse, Rochester, Medina, Lockport, Little Falls, Troy. Whether the cargo went east or west, there was plenty to be seen. The salt business and other growing enterprises of that era of expansion bred ever new and newer settlements. The boats had comfortable living quarters and a canal boatman didn't have to live alone if he didn't want to. If married, he took his wife along to steer the boat and keep house for him.

Then, passing under the canal bridge at some little town where the folks gathered and shouted greetings as the boats glided beneath, the boatmen sang:

> Low, Bridge, everybody down!
> Low, Bridge, everybody down!
> You'll always know your neighbors,
> You'll always know your gal
> If you've ever navigated
> On the Erie Canal!*

If salt was essential to the canal, the canal was no less indispensable to the growth of the salt industry. Its emergence upon a grand scale began when the loaded boats first moved on their regular schedules, carrying the cargoes to new markets as they opened up, just as James Geddes had envisioned.

---

*The old canal songs quoted here are taken from Carl Sandburg's book, "The American Song Bag," published by Harcourt Brace & Co., to whom acknowledgments are made.

CHAPTER EIGHT

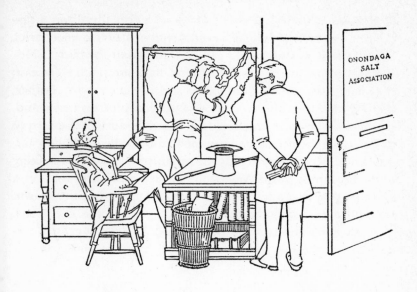

REACHING FOR THE
WESTERN MARKETS

DOWN FROM New Haven, Conn., in the early winter of 1857 came a slender, middle-aged man who showed an enormous interest in the *modus operandi* of drilling salt wells. He gave his name as Edwin L. Drake, said that he had been a New Haven Railroad conductor, and was headed for the Allegheny River valley in Pennsylvania. More than that the deponent said not. But within two years America was ringing with the name of this same Drake, and with a new-born, vigorous industry.

In Oil Creek, a minor tributary of the Allegheny River, there is, near Titusville, Pa., a small island. On that island some ugly black fluid was seeping up through a shallow spring. Some enterprising business men bottled this black oil and were selling it as a liniment under the name of "Seneca Oil"—Indians of that tribe having rubbed it on their red skins for whatever ailed them. Sometimes it was spoken of as "Pennsylvania rock oil."

Fresh from his six-months' stay in Syracuse, Drake came to the island, saw the shallow spring and began to apply drilling methods he had observed at Onondaga. William A. Smith, mechanic, who had made tools for cleaning salt wells, agreed to make Drake the necessary equipment and do the drilling.

John J. McLaurin, a local historian of Titusville, speaking of the beginning of the American petroleum industry by Drake, says that they dug a few feet around the spring, but the hole at once filled with water and caved in.

"Let's drive down some iron tubing," Drake suggested, remembering the salt wells. "We'll drill inside it and that will keep out the water."

Frederick Way, in his interesting book *The Allegheny** describes what followed:

They drilled steadily along and at 63 feet struck hard pan. As the drill pierced the rock, evidences of the presence of petroleum abounded.

"On Saturday afternoon, August 6, 1859, the well had reached a depth of 69 feet," says the McLaurin records, "and was working in coarse sand. Smith and his sons concluded to lay off until Monday morning. As they were about to quit, the drill suddenly dropped ten inches into a crevice such as was common in salt wells. Nothing was thought of this circumstance; the tools were drawn out and all hands adjourned to Titusville. Mr. Smith, however, went out to the well on Sunday afternoon. Peering into the hole, he saw fluid within eight or ten feet. A piece of tin spouting lay nearby. He plugged up one end of it, let it down by a string and pulled it up. His improvised bucket was full of petroleum!

"By noon the pumping apparatus was adjusted and the well

*Farrar & Rinehart, 1942.

commenced producing at the rate of 20 barrels a day." Before very long production had reached 600 barrels a day, refineries were put up, and prospectors were flocking by the hundreds into Oil City, Titusville, and environs.

Drake, however, couldn't stand his new-found prosperity. He went off on a spending spree which cost him many hundreds of thousands of dollars and, in time, brought him to a poverty greater than he had ever known.

Yes, there was a close interrelation between the salt and oil industries. Early salt men, seeking brine, often struck a flow of petroleum and turned away in disgust, not realizing its value. Many oil men drilling for petroleum, made the air blue with profanity when "all they got was a flow of salt brine."

The Kanawha salt industry supplied the drill which was later to make possible the growth of the petroleum industry; and Edwin Drake, the pioneer of that industry, learned how to drill oil wells from observing the Onondaga salt workers in Syracuse.

* * * *

But something had happened in Syracuse in 1821 that foreshadowed a complete metamorphosis in salt-making methods.

New York State set aside an acreage of salt land "for the experiment of making salt by solar evaporation, instead of by boiling," and as an inducement to launch such a trial balloon, offered special considerations to the launchers. Solar salt makers could produce duty-free; and there was additional legislation that promised certain other perquisites to those who would make the effort. All of which disgusted the makers of kettle salt.

A cry went up from the kettle owners that it couldn't be done. And yet there was some logic in the state's action. The state law makers were looking some years ahead. Wood, the only fuel then in use, was becoming increasingly scarce and proportionately expensive, what with the need for hauling it longer and longer distances, as the forests, mile by mile, were cut away. Bituminous and anthracite coal, in turn succeeding wood as fuel, sent the operating costs enormously high.

With reason, therefore, the Onondaga historian, Franklyn Chase, marvels that the Syracuse salt men let thirty busy years go by before letting the sun do the work gratis, just as the same

Syracuse in the Seventies — Lake Onondaga just beyond, and at your right, smoking salt works

sun had been doing the same job for centuries on the seacoast.

There was another side to the picture, however. It was common knowledge that upstate New York's sunlight is hot enough during only four or five months of the year to evaporate brine. Hence it would be necessary to make enough salt during those hot months to carry them through the cold seasons. This change would mean, too, that salt producers, if they decided to convert from kettle to solar, would have to replace their equipment with an entirely new mechanism. Still further, the end product of solar evaporation is a coarse-grained salt, such as was in great demand by packing houses and fisheries, but totally unfit for human consumption without first being put through some sort of a refining course.

The idea, for all that, stuck in the minds of the salt makers and some bold spirits began to make solar salt even while the yearly output of the kettles was still mounting steadily.

And how that kettle total had skyrocketed! In 1804 it had been 100,000 bushels. That was during the last year of Asa Danforth's superintendency of the warehouse. By 1810, the figure had mounted 400 percent. It was 526,000 in 1825, following the opening of the Erie Canal to Syracuse. Eighteen-twenty-eight saw the total bushelage top the 1,000,000 mark. That, in turn, was tripled in 1841. The same year the first solar report was issued — 220,000 bushels.

There is a mighty difference between the two: 220,000 solar versus 3,000,000 kettle. And yet, men standing by in Syracuse that year of 1841, watching the operation of both methods, would live to see the position of the two reversed.

A word about making solar salt. In this process shallow wooden vats replace iron kettles even as the sun replaces furnace fires. Werner, the New York State salt historian, explains the solar process in some detail:

Two sets of wooden vats are erected, each vat about eighteen feet wide and one foot deep, their length being governed by the space available. They are mounted on piles three or four feet above the ground.

From the reservoir comes the brine through wooden pipes to the first series of vats. There it is allowed to stand until many of the impurities sink to the bottom. Then it is let into another series or tier of vats where the sun's rays evaporate the water, leaving a clear, coarse residue of salt on the bottom of the vats. This is gathered, dried and packed for shipping.

You can see at a glance how vital a part the weather plays in such a procedure. A good hot summer—May to September—and up goes the salt yield so that all orders may be filled and a good stock kept in the state warehouse against the coming of winter. But—comes a rainy season. Production drops off and the salt makers get behind in filling their orders.

It wasn't long, though, before salt men hit upon a plan to protect the brine in the vats in case of rain, even though it meant a brief interruption of evaporation which could be resumed when the skies cleared and the sun came out again. They built a movable roof over each vat, shaped like a house gable. It moved easily on rollers and could, with a slight push, be shifted over the salt vat when rain came, and off again when the sun once more showed his smiling face.

Salt workmen, their wives and children, all had a part in solar salt making, and on each rested a certain responsibility to see that those vats were covered when the rains descended. The elderly lady, whom I have previously quoted, recalls how the arrangement extended into the schoolroom.

"Each of us children was assigned a certain number of vats and was paid a nominal sum for keeping them covered or uncovered as the weather ordered us. There was a big bell in town which a man, posted as a lookout, rang when he saw rain coming. At the sound of that bell, we children would leave our books (glad of the chance, you may be sure) and dash out of the school room. Out of the plants would come the workmen and out of their kitchens, our mothers. And such a rattling and rolling and banging as the salt covers were shifted into place, you never heard before!

"Fifteen or twenty minutes later we'd be back at our desks."

Since the vats were shallow, long and wide, the salt blocks had to cover large areas. In 1850, for example, the entire Third and Sixth Wards of old Syracuse became one great vista of far-reaching solar plants which resembled, when covered, long rows of play houses with their little gabled roofs touching. Beyond them, as far as the eye could see, were the big ponds or reservoirs where the brine was stored before evaporation.

In the two momentous decades preceding the Civil War, Syracuse developed well defined markets and trade routes. The canal boats carried salt east and west to all the cities along the Erie's length. Down at New York City, coastwise ships took it

north to New England ports and although a few local solar
plants remained, Onondaga salt found there a ready market,
despite considerable importation. The same was true as far
south as Philadelphia. These markets were secure. Canada, too,
was a dependable market. The Oswego Canal took salt boats
directly from the plants in Syracuse to Lake Ontario; there the
cargoes were transferred to lake schooners bound for neighboring
cities in the Dominion.

But in the year 1848 the eyes of the Onondaga salt men were
mainly fastened upon the West—out there beyond Buffalo and
the western terminus of the Erie Canal; out there where new
towns and cities along the lakes were springing up with each
passing month; out there where was a flourishing new community at the head of Lake Michigan—Chicago.

By 1848, burly, boisterous, bustling, little more than a large
frontier town, Chicago had nevertheless wealth, boundless energy and room in which to expand. More, too, it was located
at the point where a new canal, running from Lake Michigan,
cut across the State of Illinois to the Mississippi River Valley.

The association of salt men at Syracuse, keen on the scent of
new markets, had been watching Chicago for some time and
waiting for the completion of this Illinois & Michigan Canal.
In their office on South Salina Street in Syracuse, they dis-
cussed it.

"That ditch is going to mean a lot more business for us,"
said one association member, studying the map of the states.
"That'll give us a water route clear down to St. Louis to connect
with the steamboat traffic. See there! We can ship up the Mississippi River to the Falls of St. Anthony. Down the Mississippi
and up the Ohio. . . ."

"Hold on!" another member broke in, tracing the course of
the rivers with his finger. "Don't forget Kanawha. Those fellows
down there in Virginia have got the Ohio and the lower Mississippi trade all sewed up. Oh, I know we move a little salt down
to Pittsburgh by shallow bateaux on Beaver River. But those

Kanawha fellows furnish all the salt to the packing houses at Cincinnati—more than a million bushels a year. We can't buck them! What I'm thinking about is that country out there beyond Chicago—west of it. That's where we'll get our new business. T'other side of St. Louis and the Mississippi and farther up the river. . . . You know what we ought to do? We ought to have a representative in Chicago."

And so it was that in 1848 a young man named Alonzo Richmond came out to Chicago from Syracuse and opened up an office. The name over the door was

> ### RICHMOND & COMPANY
> *Agents for Onondaga Salt*

A modest little office it was, near the docks on Chicago River where the lake schooners and an occasional wheezing sidewheel steamer came in to dock. But it wasn't long before this little salt agency began to attract attention.

Salt being a commodity that everybody had to have, Chicago merchants soon found it extremely convenient to place their orders with Richmond & Company, certain that they would be attended to promptly. In fact, Richmond & Company usually kept a pretty good stock in barrels right there in their own Chicago warehouse to supply the current demand. The larger orders, of course, went at once out to Onondaga, by ship over the lakes to Buffalo, thence by fast canal packet to Syracuse. There the order was filled and the salt followed the return route by which the order had been sent in.

Remember this little salt agency in Chicago: Richmond & Company. Soon it would be known as Richmond & Comstock and it is vital to the American epic of producing and distributing salt on a national scale. In time it would evolve into a mighty organization whose name would be known in millions of American households.

Back in Syracuse, side by side, the making of kettle and solar salt went on; the solar product called "coarse salt," the kettle known to the trade as "fine salt." Year by year, however, old Sol was doing a bigger job and the number of vats was gradually catching up with the kettles.

They knew—these Syracuse salt makers—what a canal can do for an industry such as theirs which shipped great quantities of a bulk commodity, and for the growth of a new community. Had not their own Erie Canal, planned largely and brought to reality by James Geddes, one of their own kind, made possible the cheap and dependable shipment of salt? Had not the whole of New York State profited by it? By the same token, they knew, the new channel at Chicago, joining the Great Lakes with the Mississippi River system, would advance their own interests and those of the rising city of Chicago to still greater heights of commercial importance.

The old pump at the Syracuse Salt Works.

CHAPTER NINE

"THAT STRONG RED SALT
FROM KANAWHA"

YOU HAVEN'T FORGOTTEN that buffalo lick in the Kanawha Valley where the Indians took Mary Ingles to make salt in 1755? It lay for years afterwards deserted save for occasional visits of woodsmen, both red and white, and of wild animals whose trails led to it out of the woods from three points of the compass.

Sixteen miles down the river at the mouth of a little stream since named Coal River, a few settlers made camp in the year 1760, soon replacing their tents with log houses. Desperately in need of salt, they sent two of their strong young men in dugout canoes paddling up to the lick to bring back a supply. These lads simply filled their canoes with salt brine, drifted down again to their comrades; then they boiled the brine. For some years this seems to have been a popular way of getting salt to scattered settlements.

Next, following the close of the Revolution, two names appear in Kanawha annals, which for the ensuing century and a half were a part of salt history—Dickinson and Ruffner. There was a "John Dickinson, Salter," listed as a subscriber to *"Lexicon Technicum"*—universal English dictionary of arts and sciences, published in London, 1604. On the same page is listed the name of Isaac Newton.

A later John Dickinson came west over the hills from the Shenandoah Valley and settled in Kanawha in 1785. He bought up the land containing the buffalo lick, as well as another and very mysterious salt spring which was never still. It bubbled away unceasingly. From it issued a strange deep-earthy smell. When you happened to strike a light with your flint and steel, the whole spring caught fire and blazed up.

George Washington, who had owned much Kanawha real estate and was selling it off through agents at a fair profit, had once owned this burning spring. He called it a "salt bituminous spring," and said that it burned continually; not knowing, of course, that natural gas, as well as salt, was present in this valley and some day would be put to use for the benefit of the entire region.

Those were days of sizeable real estate transactions. Before long we find John Dickinson, a farmer at heart who never got around to making salt at the lick, selling five hundred acres of his holdings for £500 sterling to Joseph Ruffner. The buffalo lick went with it.

"It's my intention," said Ruffner, "to make salt and sell it. We've got a growing settlement here and I know we can find a good market."

But old Joseph Ruffner died shortly, and his sons presently took up the task of making salt. Meanwhile, Elisha Brooks had beaten them to it. Brooks sank a shallow well near the Ruffner holdings and found brine. He then set to work to build a plant. He had a couple of dozen small iron kettles and could get a bushel of salt from 500 gallons of brine, according to Atkinson's

"History of Kanawha County." Dr. John Hale, Mary Ingles' great grandson and archivist of Kanawha Valley, says that Brooks "placed his kettles in a double row with a flue beneath, a chimney at one end, a firebox at the other."

Where did Brooks learn the technique? Is it possible that he visited Onondaga, where only seven years earlier, as explained in another chapter, DeWitt and VanVleck had set their kettles in a double row in exactly the same manner? Possible, but hardly probable. People didn't get around much in those days. Most likely Brooks read of the process in *Niles Register,* an early gazetteer in which business men of that day placed great reliance. To get his brine, Brooks had to sink several hollowed logs, eight or ten feet long. This kept out fresh earth water and allowed the brine to well up from the bottom. Into these he dipped his buckets by means of a "well swape" (sweep). Even so, Brooks was making about 150 pounds of salt per day and selling it to his neighbors for ten cents per pound.

"As our salt comes from the earth," wrote Hale of the Kanawha salt, "it holds some carbonate of iron in solution. When boiled, this iron becomes oxidized and gives a reddish tinge to the brine." For all that, Hale continues, "Kanawha salt soon acquired a reputation for its strong pungent taste and its superior quality for curing meat, butter, etc." Therefore, many people who used it recognized these qualities in connection with its color and before long orders were coming in from far and near for that "strong, red salt from Kanawha."

It was 1806 when Joseph Ruffner's two sons, David and young Joseph, set seriously to work. They felt that Brooks' "red salt" was not the best the Valley could yield. A cleaner and clearer product was what they wanted and they determined to bore deeper into the earth to get it.

The buffalo lick and its environs was now a flat, trampled muddy plain, many rods in extent, on the north shore of the Kanawha River. Behind it lay a hollow in the hill known as Thoroughfare Gap, so well had it been trampled by visiting animals. Right in the middle of the Gap an old settler by the name of Daniel Boone had his cabin. Not only was Boone a mighty hunter; he was also a mighty salt maker and never failed, in passing between Richmond and the "dark and bloody ground" of Kentucky, to stop in Kanawha and make himself a supply. At this time he was living there and representing the wild frontier county of Kanawha in the State Legislature at Richmond. No one watched the Ruffners' endeavor with keener interest than the renowned old frontiersman.

"If you can reach the bottom of all this infernal mud and mire, you'll hit stronger brine," said Boone.

"But how are we going to do that?" Joseph Ruffner inquired. Dr. Hale describes how they answered that question:

"They provided a straight, well-formed, hollow sycamore tree, four feet in diameter, sawed off square at one end. This is technically known as a 'gum.' They set it upright, the large end down, held perpendicular by props and braces on four sides. A platform, on which two men could stand, was fixed about the top of the gum. Then a swape or sweep (a large lever) was erected, having a fulcrum in a forked post set in the ground.

"They made a bucket from half of a whiskey barrel. They attached it by a rope to the business end of the swape and fastened also a rope to the long end to raise and lower the bucket. With one man inside the gum, armed with a short pick, shovel and crowbar, two men on the platform to draw up and empty and return the bucket, and three or four to work the swape, crew and outfit were complete."

It must have been mighty crowded quarters in which to work— that four foot gum. But digging went forward and as the earth was hoisted up, the gum sank down into the ground. Thirteen feet down, it reached what seemed to be solid rock. This proved to be only a crust of shale, six inches thick. To their disgust, the Ruffners found below it a weaker brine than was at the surface.

Undiscouraged, they sank another well, a hundred feet back

from the river shore. Forty-five feet down, using one gum placed on top of another, they came to the same bed of sand and gravel as that upon which they started at the other well.

"Here's where we came in," the Ruffners must have said. But still they did not give up. Solid rock, they knew, could not be far below.

"To penetrate this bed," says Dr. Hale, "they bored a three and one-half inch tube through a long straight log, using a shanked auger to do the job. Then they sharpened one end of it and shod it with iron. This they hammered into the ground, pile-driver fashion; let down a glass vial and brought up a sampling of the brine."

Alas! It was only slightly brackish, hardly briny at all.

Back to well Number One to have still another try. They reached bedrock. Then, using crude but tough hand-forged augers, they penetrated the rock, discovering that salt water seeped through the layers of the rock itself. In smaller quantities it is true; but the brine was much stronger. With great difficulty and by using some of the most outlandish makeshifts, they got down as far as their tube would let them.

"And now what?" asked David Ruffner. "We can't blast a hole down there under that water."

His brother said they would try everything until they hit upon a way of keeping out fresh water.

Old residents of Charleston and Malden in the Kanawha Valley still repeat the story of the difficulties the Ruffners encountered in bringing in the first deep salt well; how they overcame obstacles which would have baffled less bullheaded prospectors. How to make a gum fit on to the rocks snugly to keep out fresh water and at the same time allow the brine to come up from below? How to join one tube to another as the boring progressed, protect the joints, keep it dry inside? How to turn the augers from the surface of the ground while the bits were working in solid rock? How to get enough of the strong brine oozing from the rock to make salt on a profitable basis? How to—How to—.

It was one unending, irritating problem for more than a year of endeavor.

One day in 1807, their hand-turned augers, slowly revolving sixteen feet within the rock, struck a cavity and the flow of brine increased greatly. Still they continued their boring, the strength of the flow mounting the farther they went.

What they needed now was a long metal tube—something no blacksmith shop within five hundred miles could produce. For a substitute, they fitted together two slender grooved timbers, like the halves of a giant pencil with the lead space three inches in diameter. They wound it tightly round with tarred twine and used that as a pipe to bring out the brine.

And so the Kanawha salt industry, second only to Onondaga in importance, got slowly under way, the Brooks' and Ruffner furnaces being the first on the job.

Here you see the inside of a salt "block" in Syracuse more than three-quarters of century ago.

CHAPTER TEN

THE LONG AUGERS
OF TOBIAS RUFFNER

ELISHA BROOKS' first salt works could make a bushel of salt from 500 gallons of brine drawn from above bedrock. David and Joseph Ruffner, bringing out brine from rock itself, could make a bushel from 200 gallons. The matter did not rest there, for the two Ruffners had a younger brother, Tobias by name, who really set the Kanawha salt industry going in a big way.

"The fertile genius of Tobias Ruffner," wrote the historian Atkinson, "brought to light the untold riches—the great saline reservoir—hidden *beneath* the deep stratum of rock which underlies Kanawha County and its alluvial bottom land, and, indeed, a large section of the West." (Atkinson, remember, was referring to the "West" of 1809).

Tobias had no college education, but he possessed a mind as keen as the tool he perfected. He watched his kinsmen and other salt prospectors making their initial drillings and using up so great a quantity of brine to produce so meager a quantity of salt.

Omen of ill-luck! The over-turned salt cellar before Judas Iscariot, in Da Vinci's painting "The Last Supper."

Lot's wife was turned to salt, as recorded in the Old Testament, and as pictured here by Dore's famous engraving.

Old office of the New York State Salt Springs, Syracuse, about 1860.

Loading salt on the Erie Canal, Syracuse, about 1860.

Loading salt from Syracuse's Solar vats, 1870.

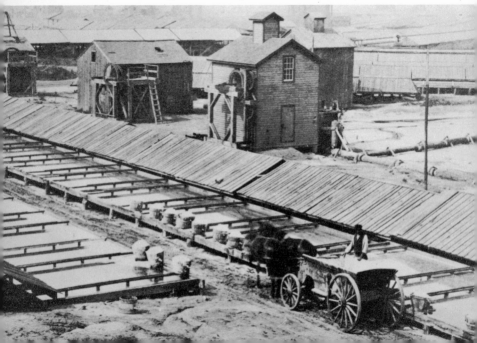

"If the strength of the brine increases the farther you go into that rock, it must be good and strong underneath it," he told his brothers. They laughed at him.

"You fool!" his friends told him, "You can't bore clean through that rock. It's the bottom of the valley."

Tobias grinned. "Maybe," he said.

People began to talk about "Ruffner's folly," as they watched Tobias and his men drilling day after day. He had hammered out in his own blacksmith shop a new type of auger. He had leased the site of one of his brother's abandoned wells. And now he was boring for all he was worth. The sharp bits, made of wrought iron, bored gradually into the rock; the shanks were pieced together as the boring went on.

Finding human muscle-power too slow to work his augers, Tobias rigged up a horse-turned mill and continued going down. One hundred feet, two hundred, three hundred—with the cost piling up with each succeeding foot. And then suddenly, at 410 feet, "the workman who was putting his weight on the auger as the horse turned it, felt it give way under him and plunge downward without resistance."

When he withdrew it, out spurted a thick stream of brine like blood from an artery, save that it was not red, but clear and sparkling.*

Tobias tested this brine from below bedrock. It was found to yield a bushel of clear, white salt from 45 gallons. No more talk now of the "red salt of Kanawha!"

The discovery electrified the county and apparently everybody who owned land along the river shores set to work punching holes in the ground to find brine. And furnaces started popping up at intervals like king-size crawfish "castles."

---

*The two historians from whom I have taken this information on early Kanawha salt making—Hale and Atkinson—are recognized authorities in their field—history. Certain modern technically-trained salt men, however, question the accuracy of their description of Tobias Ruffner's tapping the "great subterranean salt lake" to which they refer. Tobias undoubtedly did bring in the strong brine which resulted in the growth of the Kanawha Valley's salt industry; but definitely not—contend the moderns—in so dramatic a manner as that recorded!

The strength of this Kanawha brine varies according to localities, Dr. Hale explains. "The range," he says, "may be stated at, say, 6 to 12 degrees by the salometer, Baume Scale (distilled water being 0 degrees, saturation 25 degrees). But the average strength of the Valley's brine from which salt is made is about 8 or 10 degrees."

By 1817, thirty furnaces were smoking away and the salt was moving out in a steady stream. That year Kanawha sent out 700,000 bushels. By 1832 the output had topped a million bushels. During the Mexican War it reached two and three-quarter millions; dropped again, to rise in 1850 above three million.

But it was the War of the States that, as we shall see later, brought Kanawha to the peak of its production.

And here in Kanawha we find the name of George H. Patrick of Onondaga. Patrick had invented an evaporating pan which he tried to introduce in the Syracuse salt industry. The salt makers there, however seem not to have shown much interest in his pan; but when an invitation from Kanawha came to Patrick in 1833, he moved South bag and baggage and before long had induced practically every Kanawha furnace to replace their kettles with his pans.

Patrick's invention was so well received in Kanawha that he settled there. His descendants are in Kanawha to this day.

There also was Uncle Billy Morris. Uncle Billy was a successful well borer but his name is all but forgotten, though the entire American petroleum industry has reason to remember his invention of a salt-well drilling machine that reached new depths. He called his invention simply "slips." It was a long, double link with close-fitting jaws which could slide loosely up and down. Fashioned of the best steel, thirty inches long, fitted top and bottom with pin and socket joints, "these slips are interposed between the heavy iron sinker with its cutting edge pointed down and the line of auger poles above." This gives the heavy sinker and bit, Hale explains, a clean, quick-cutting plunge. It was a mighty forward step in well drilling.

Dr. Hale's big salt furnace at Snow Hill on the Kanawha

Billy Morris, well borer, never asked for or received any patent for his "slips." He lived to see the day, however, when the new petroleum industry adopted it universally and found it to their great advantage. It enabled well borers to reach 2,000 feet in the Kanawha Valley and bring up a splendid brine.

*   *   *   *

Into the office of Colonel Lewis Ruffner, a relative of Tobias, and one of the larger Kanawha salt operators, walked an intelligent-faced, upstanding Negro youth on a day in the later 1860's. The Colonel, always on the lookout for good laborers, asked his name.

"Booker," the boy answered.

"Booker? — Booker what?" The Colonel was familiar with the

custom of most Negroes in those days when slavery had but recently been sent to the discard, to take the name of their late masters. Booker, however (as he later recounted it), had a different idea. Quickly he cast about in his mind for the greatest name he could possibly think of—the father of his country—and then answered:

"Booker—uh—uh—Washington."

He got the job.

It was pretty strenuous work—rolling out loaded salt barrels and placing them on a slide or chute for loading on to steamboat decks.

This chute was a unique gadget. It was so arranged that it would fill up with barrels nearly to the top, but it had a curved-up bottom. Placing one more barrel at the top sent the bottom barrel rolling onto the steamboat deck making room for another at the top. It was a good system of loading and saved a lot of back-breaking effort and a lot of broken barrels. Before long Booker had given such a good account of himself that the Colonel found him indispensable.

But the salt works could not hold the boy. If anyone had told him he was slated for the Hall of Fame and other well-deserved honors at the hand of his country as the greatest educator of his own people, he would not then have believed it.

He had tramped all the way from Franklin County in old Virginia to work in Kanawha. When he had earned enough money, he sent back for his mother. And long after her son had gone from Kanawha to Hampton Institute and had become well known to the American lecture platform, respected by North and South alike, this aged colored woman persisted in keeping a little restaurant in the venerable town of Malden (Kanawha Salines), near the Ruffner ancestral home. There, traveling salesmen would stop to eat of her home-cooked meals.

Sometime early in the present century President Theodore Roosevelt entertained Booker Washington at dinner at the White House.

"What did your son talk to the President about, Aunt Jane?" one of the salesman asked.

"Ain't talk 'bout nuttin—jes et!" the quick answer came back.

As I write this page in the spring of 1947, the National Government has just minted a memorial half-dollar in honor of the 100th birthday anniversary of the former salt boy of Kanawha; and his bust stands in the Hall of Fame.

Kanawha's salt industry today is represented by one lone furnace. Within a mile or two of where the first buffalo lick drew to it herds of wild animals; where long ago Mary Ingles made her first salt; where Daniel Boone once had his cabin—there Charles C. Dickinson, descendant of the pioneer of that name, operates, among his various other activities, an evaporating-pan furnace. Annually it turns out about fifty thousand barrels which find ready market in adjacent agricultural areas.

Recently I stood with Mr. Dickinson in the midst of this former seat of national salt making, and watched his furnace puffing busily away at its chore. Aloof, it sits among the Kanawha Valley's long string of chemical plants and allied operations (they have located here because of the same brine which built the salt furnaces) that have made our valley increasingly important in America's industrial picture.

As I stood there, I could see the Kanawha River still flowing placidly along. Comfortable old homes of aged dignity remain along Malden's tree-lined streets. I tried to conjure up a picture of our valley as it had been in the days when both shores of the river smoked with a half-hundred busy furnaces; when the river channel was a panorama of loaded salt boats making their way down stream with the current and of occasional steamboats arriving and departing.

That was the picture I retained from what the old men had told me in my boyhood, as they sat reminiscing in Doctor Rogers' drugstore in Charleston. But it was uphill work—trying to recreate a mental photograph of an industry you have never actually seen. So I gave it up as a bad job. Nevertheless the tradition is there, and the authenticated old records bear testimony of Kanawha's vital part in the progressive history of making salt.

Other pages in this book explain why the industry there eventually expired.

Home of an old Kanawha salt maker.

CHAPTER ELEVEN

WHERE "BIG BUSINESS" GOT ITS START

THE PEOPLE of Kanawha Valley in Virginia were predominantly Southern in sentiment, many of them slaveholders; and, following the War of the States, of strong Democratic persuasion. They have, in the main, opposed big business, Wall Street, and that indefinite thing known as "monopoly" or "trusts."

And yet—believe it, it's true!—right there in the Kanawha Valley was born America's first trust, the Nation's earliest example of big business in a monopolistic sense. That occurred some years before John D. Rockefeller, generally thought of as the originator of the trusts, had donned his first diapers.

Who started this trust? None but the Kanawha salt makers, if you please! Its object—they made no bones about it—was to keep prices up by keeping production down; by buying up all the salt lands and by paying other producers, not members of their league, to keep out of the "profession."

The irony of it!—right there in Ole Virginia. And I do mean

"ole"—1817. It's almost as cockeyed as the fact that the Onondaga salt men in upstate New York, supposed stronghold of wealth and rugged individualism, made salt under strict state supervision.

About this Kanawha salt trust: A score of leading salt manufacturers organized themselves into the Kanawha Salt Company in 1817. They were determined to limit the quantity of salt to be produced in the several years following. The articles of agreement, entered into November 10, 1817, state that certain salt manufacturers whose names were given, "do for the purpose of manufacturing and disposing of salt on general and uniform plan and method, form themselves into a company under the name and style of the Kanawha Salt Company and for the government and management of their affairs, do adopt the following articles: . . ."

Briefly, the agreement provided that the company should start business on January 1, 1818, and expire December 31, 1822. It created a board of directors to have charge of the company's business and specified the method of their election and terms of office. The president and directors were to receive all salt made by the members of the company, to regulate and fix the price from time to time, sell the salt on terms to be made by them and make a fair division of the net proceeds of all salt sales among the members of the company in proportion to their holdings in it.

The members had to deliver to the company's warehouse each month all the salt they produced, packed in barrels. They were given credit on the company's books. A member had better not try to lease or transfer his furnace to any person not a member of the "company," without permission of the board. It wouldn't be healthy for him. The use of tallow to clear the brine was prohibited, under penalty, in making salt. Here is Article VIII of the regulations:

"The quantity of salt to be manufactured by all subscribers in the year One Thousand Eight Hundred and Eighteen shall not exceed Four Hundred and Fifty Thousand bushels and the proportional quantity to be manufactured by each subscriber, or any person or persons manufacturing for or under them, or any of them, shall not exceed the following quantities, to wit:

	Bushels		Bushels
Daniel Ruffner	9,000	Aaron Stockton	20,000
Joseph Lovell	25,000	John Reynolds	12,000
Tobias Ruffner	9,000	Stephen Ratcliff	10,000
David Ruffner	40,000	John, Samuel and	
William Steele (of Ky.)	20,000	John D. Shrewsbury	30,000
Leonard and Charles Morris	33,000	Andrew Donally	40,000
William Steele & Co.	53,000	John J. Cabell	20,000
Charles Brown	16,000	Isaac and Bradford Noyes	30,000

(This was an average cut of about 50% for each subscriber.)

There was a heavy penalty for making more than the amount assigned. By mutual agreement, certain markets were assigned to each member. Article XII of this agreement is most interesting:

"As it is suggested that there is too great a quantity of salt being manufactured for the demand, the subscribers hereby engage to take all proper means in their power to lessen the quantity to be manufactured by themselves and others."

For the first five years of its existence, the Kanawha Salt Company rode the crest of the wave. Its members made money and the salt poured from its furnaces on boats down the rivers to service the towns and cities of the South and Southwest. (That was before the rise of the packing-house industry at Cincinnati.) Over the old State Road (now known as the Midland Trail) — the famous highway laid out on paths made by the buffalo— mountain wagons took salt loads to the eastern and southeastern cities.

Startling evidence of the effect of transportation on the cost of salt in those days is illustrated by the following examples: At Kanawha Salines, for a time, you could buy salt at twenty cents per bushel. If you bought it at Lewisburg (White Sulphur Springs), 125 miles to the east, it cost you fifty cents a bushel; in Charlottesville, sixty cents per bushel, and so on; the farther away from the source you went the higher the price, until the initial cost of the salt was entirely lost sight of in the piling up of transportation charges.

Opposition to the trust naturally arose and in time killed it. But in 1826 and several times subsequently through the years, similar salt monopolies rose in Kanawha. To silence opposition, in the decades 1840-1870 the Kanawha Salt Company began the practice of "dead-renting" furnaces of non-members. That meant simply paying their competitors a good round sum to shut down their furnaces and go on home. John Q. Dickinson, one of the most important salt men of the valley, refused to join the trust and dead-rented his plant. He was a grandson of one of the founders of the salt industry and his grandson in turn operates today the sole remaining furnace in the Kanawha Valley.

Parenthetically, my own grandfather, as it happened, owned two salt furnaces; one at High Bank and the other at Snow Hill, both within a mile or two of the old buffalo lick. He, too, refused to "jine up" with the trust. He accepted, however, the sum of $4,500 annually for each of his furnaces—in other words, dead-renting them. Being in the not-making-salt business, he found, wasn't so bad after all, for that was a lot of money in those days. Farmers, in recent years, have had something of the same experience when Government subsidies got in their licks.

It was during this latter period, 1840-1860, that John P. Hale, Mary Ingles' great grandson, became head of the Kanawha salt trust, and production reached its peak of almost 4,000,000 bushels annually.

This Dr. Hale was a most remarkable man. He was an inventive genius of America's great era of expansion. Before petroleum had been found near Titusville, Pennsylvania, Hale had developed a process of making oil from cannel coal in Kanawha Valley, distilling it by the retort process. He laid the first brick pavement in the United States, using paving blocks which he himself manufactured in Charleston. He built a fleet of steamboats to move salt to the Cincinnati packing houses and to carry passengers also. And—oh, yes, one other thing—it was he who brought the English sparrows to the United States in the belief that they would be a pleasant addition to America's bird life.

Hale lived to see his salt business die out; to see the first motor cars which would demand smooth-surface highways rather than his brick paved roads; to see his cannel coal oil (once it sold for 85c a gallon) a drug on the market in the face of natural petroleum products. Only his sparrows remained—increasing by the billion each decade without ever putting a penny in his or anyone else's pocket.

Getting back to salt making: Two well-known salt men, Tompkins and Shrewsbury, were boring a new well along about this period, not far from the "burning spring" which George Washington once owned. They had great difficulty in bringing in the brine. They would bore until evening and then light a torch to work by. After several weeks' effort, Shrewsbury swore late one evening: "I'll strike that brine today, or hell!"

Chug! Chug! Chug! the boring went on. Suddenly the augers hit a pocket of natural gas and—Wham! Out flew the augers, the heavy iron bit and sinker, and almost five hundred pounds of auger poles. The gas caught fire from the torch.

"Well, I guess it's hell!" Tompkins shouted back over his shoulder.

A column of brine followed, too, according to Atkinson, and stood 150 feet high. The roaring of the gas and the water could be heard for miles.

"There's enough natural gas there to light the entire city of London or Paris," remarked visiting scientists.

But the salt men thought only of the brine which they could not bring under control for some weeks.

At last the fire was put out. While this well was still blowing, however, stage drivers through the Kanawha Valley would stop to let their passengers view the great natural wonder—a salt well spouting a stream that must have looked like Old Faithful geyser. One day a Harvard Professor came through and with thorough scientific curiosity, he struck a light to see if it would burn. He found out. All the newly re-erected machinery and scaffolding was blown away. The blaze singed the Professor's eyebrows and hair; set his clothes on fire. He ran and jumped in the Kanawha River and was duly fished out. They put him on the stage and sent him down to Charleston six miles away for medical treatment.

Colonel Dickinson, one of the owners of the well, sent his agent to see the Professor.

"Go and have that Harvard fellow arrested! I'll have the law on him—that is, unless you find he is such a damn fool he didn't know any better."

The Colonel's agent delivered the message.

"It's a pretty hard alternative," growled the Harvard man. "Under the circumstances, however, I confess under the latter clause."

The Colonel was so delighted to hear a Harvard Professor confess to anything, that he promptly forgot the whole matter.

As a postscript to this incident, Tompkins and Shrewsbury turned the natural gas to good account. They used it as fuel to boil their brine. Here was the first use of natural gas industrially in the United States. It bade fair to throw both wood and coal into the discard as fuel not only for salt making but for other industrial purposes throughout a wide area.

Meanwhile other events were shaping in the salt world; and the Kanawha industry, although none of the manufacturers then realized it, was already on the decline.

CHAPTER TWELVE

ONONDAGA 1850 KANAWHA

SALTVILLE

SALT SITUATION AT
MID-CENTURY

HERE, THEN, is the picture of America's system of salt supply about the middle of the last century.

Syracuse, with its 4,000,000-bushel annual output was serving the northern states, nearby Canada and a new western market just coming alive beyond the upper Mississippi River.

The Kanawha Valley of (West) Virginia shipped a yearly output of almost 3,000,000 bushels to the middle South and the Southwest—mainly via the Ohio and Mississippi Rivers and their tributaries, a large block of the total going to the flourishing packing houses of Cincinnati.

Saltville, in the southwestern extremity of old Virginia, found its product most in demand among the farmers and planters of southern Virginia, Tennessee, the Carolinas, Georgia, and Alabama. Sometimes, though, venturing farther afield in search of business, flatboatmen would load up salt barrels on shallow-draft flatboats which would negotiate the tricky currents of four rivers. Down the Holston, the Tennessee, the Ohio, and the

Mississippi, Saltville salt would sometimes find buyers two thousand miles from base.

These were the "big three" of American salt making as of 1850. Competitors all, each frequently infringing upon the others' territory when occasion offered, but all three having one common enemy that caused them no end of irritation.

That enemy was imported salt.

More than 10,000,000 bushels, says Ella C. Lonn, historian, of Goucher College, was yearly finding its way into American ports from England, the West Indies, and other countries. Worse luck, it could be sold at a price to compete with the domestic article.

To illustrate: as Syracuse salt approached the Eastern sea-board, it found its total sales somewhat cut into by this foreign competition. Kanawha salt, headed down the Mississippi, at Memphis ran into imported salt coming upstream on steamboats from New Orleans, to whose wharves foreign ships had brought it. Saltville, meanwhile, with its 500,000-bushel output, experienced the same sort of rivalry when shipped to points near the southeastern ports. Saltville, however, suffered less since her main trade was then largely agricultural and close at hand.

Not that these were the only inland salt-producing centers before the year 1850. Far from it. There most certainly had been others; a few of them remained. But for reasons soon explained most of these lesser operations had ceased to exist. Nor was there at that time any handwriting on the wall to foretell that the "big three" themselves were all slated for something like oblivion within the next fifty years when newer and different salt fields would open up, and improved methods of manufacture and distribution come into being.

During the years that Onondaga salt was building a city, digging a canal, and servicing a large part of the Nation, neighboring New York counties had not been idle. The salt rush was on! Cayuga County, dividing Onondaga from the easternmost of the lovely Finger Lakes, started as early as 1811. And who, think you, headed it? None other than our old friend, Colonel Comfort Tyler, salt pioneer of Salina. Returning without honors from Aaron Burr's unsucessful junta, Tyler settled at the little town of Montezuma in Cayuga. Apparently he had learned of salt springs in that area years earlier but not until 1811 did he set to in earnest.

Experienced surveyor that he was, Tyler began building, first of all, an extensive network of roads to connect Montezuma with the other county villages and with the surrounding countryside. He bridged the Seneca and Clyde Rivers and the wide-spreading marshlands which covered nearly the entire county. "You could stick a surveyor's pole into those marshes," it was said, "and not hit bottom." But so skilled an engineer was Tyler that the roads he built for the purpose of hauling out the salt he intended to make are still in use.

"A gallon of our brine provides twenty ounces of salt," Tyler boasted; and the much-elected DeWitt Clinton, New York's Governor, explained: "The principal salt well that supplies Tyler's establishment is located in a bed of a fresh water creek. He extracts the salt from below the waters of this stream."

Tyler and some other Cayuga salt prospectors went in for deep boring, as the term was understood in those days. The deeper the boring, of course, the stronger the brine, a fact which encouraged them to believe that, somewhere down there, they would find a layer of "fossil salt."

Tyler's company failed. Expense of production, lack of adequate machinery and long-range transportation facilities—these caused the collapse. The wooden tubes used to carry the brine from wells to works were so leaky that the brine was weakened appreciably by the in-seeping of fresh water. Hence, by 1840 Cayuga's total had shrunk to a trickle of 18,000 bushels a year.

Neither had the neighboring counties of Wayne, Delaware, and Monroe, in all of which for a time efforts were made to produce salt profitably, worked with any marked success. The brine in each case was weaker than Onondaga's.

Genesee County's little salt industry rose, produced from a very strong brine for a short time, and died. Livingston County, just south of Onondaga, had her early salt makers, too. They were active for a time, but scheduled for an early demise.

None could compete with the well-established, great industry of Onondaga. By 1850 all had bowed out more or less gracefully, leaving the field clear to the Syracuse men. Rock salt did indeed lie under New York, in nearby Wyoming, Tompkins, and Schuyler Counties. Within the next half century it would write the first letter in the epitaph of the salt industry on the shores of once dark Onondaga Lake.

Kentucky, too, had her early salt springs and furnaces. At Big Bone Lick, where Mary Ingles had once made salt for her Indian captors, a little salt works sprang up as early as 1792. It had 104 kettles, employed nine wagons, "many horses and gear." There seems to have been a curative value in the salt waters of Big Bone—or so many people of that day thought. Like a miniature French Lick, Big Bone became a watering place for people seeking relief from illness. A picturesque place it must have been, around 1815, with its rows of cottages and shaded walks bordered with enormous mastodon ribs standing like pillars as testimony to much earlier visitors, and the salt spring gushing from the hillside. Clarke Firestone, in his engaging book "Bubbling Waters," explains how the salt water still flows as it did in times past, though nobody pays any attention to it today.

At Mann's Lick, Mayslick, Boonesborough, Goose Creek, and Lower Blue Lick, as well as several smaller springs, salt plants arose, operated, died, but during their heydey they served a purpose. This, mark you, was long before the meat-packing industry had been dreamed of. Yet Kentucky farmers were even then salting Kentucky side meat with Kentucky salt and sending it floating downstream on flatboats to New Orleans (1795).

Advertised James Morrison in the Kentucky Gazette: "I have 30,000 pounds of cured meat for sale,"—cured, he points out— "with good old Kentucky salt and meant for our Southern trade."

The same paper lists among the commodities shipped down the rivers from Louisville by barge and flatboat in 1801, 92,000 pounds of pork; 91,000 pounds of bacon; 14,000 pounds of dried salted beef, with numerous tubs of lard and butter. And all, insists the writer, cured with good old Kentucky salt. Moreover, a part of the Kentucky salt output itself went downriver.

Came 1840 and the Kentucky salt industry was doomed. The brine from which it was made was too weak to compete with Kanawha salt, obtained by deep boring, and now coming steadily down the river on steamboats.

One of the last of the famous Kentucky salt-well diggers advertised his craftsmanship in the *Kentucky Gazette* through the medium of poetry, if such indeed it may be called. A reckless rhymer, John Shaw nevertheless made himself clear:

> John Robert Shaw, who now excells
> In blowing rocks and digging wells
> Can water find by this new art—
> As well the fresh, as well the salt.

> Since conjurers became so wise
> In telling where salt water lies,
> In hopes that I'll not be forsook,
> I've tried the art of Dr. Cook.*

> No stipend of my friends I take,
> I show them all for friendship sake;
> Then all that wish to dig salt wells,
> May easy learn that Shaw excells.

By the 1840's Kentucky's entire salt production amounted to not more than a mere trickle of a few thousand bushels annually. . . .

Pick up a map of the United States and you will notice how the shapes of many of the older states—those along the Atlantic

---

*Probably refers to a scientist of the Onondaga salt region.

seaboard and as far west as the Ohio River—are irregular in comparison with those states admitted subsequently to the Union. In a peculiar way, the early salt springs of Ohio and other states included in the Northwest Territory are mixed up in this matter of laying out the lines of new states.

It was under an act of May, 1796, authorizing the sale of public lands in the new Northwest Territory, that every Government surveyor was required to note down in his field book the true location of every salt spring, with special emphasis upon the "well-known salt spring on the Scioto River."

That same act is also the basis of our present national system of rectangular surveying—that is, along the parallels of latitude and meridians of longitude, rather than by metes and bounds: e.g., from a gum tree stump, 30 poles north to a chestnut tree, thence ninety poles east to a rock, or similar unstable landmarks.

Ohio, admitted to the Union in 1802, rode in on the crest of a wave of salt-making. Salt was so scarce in Ohio that commanders of troops stationed throughout the territory kept writing back East for new supplies to be sent via packhorses. Then, in the Scioto Valley, near Zanesville, on Salt Creek, in Jackson County, and at several other places, white men followed the Indians' custom of dipping out brine. In a very few years a string of little furnaces were wheezing away—before the new century was out of its swaddling clothes.

And the State of Ohio, even as did New York, took over control of the lands on which the springs were located and leased them to private producers. Between the years 1806 and 1808 Ohio's first salt-making spree reached its pinnacle. Twenty furnaces, each with its quota of small boiling kettles, hit an all-time high of 120 bushels per week. But since only the weak, superficial brines (those found above the mantle rock) were available, 700 gallons were required to make a single bushel of salt. The brine was far weaker than seawater.

It is no wonder then that we find the State Legislature in 1818 announcing sadly that salt production was no longer profitable and asking Congress to sell off the salt lands. The request was not granted until 1822, and in 1824 the lands were finally sold.

Thus died Ohio's primary effort at salt production. That weak brine could never compete with Kanawha's product of deep boring. Yet, strange are the tricks of time! Within less than half a century another salt field—Pomeroy Bend on the Ohio River— would begin to produce a brine strong enough to compete both with Kanawha and Syracuse. And still later rock salt beds beneath the city of Cleveland on the shores of Lake Erie, and in the vicinity of Akron would yeild a yearly output greater than the total of all that Ohio made during the first two decades of the century.

A deep depression in the land, shaped like a half moon, fifteen feet deep, though some thousands of years ago it must have been much deeper, and a hundred yards long—such is the Half Moon Lick near the old site of Shawneetown, Illinois. Right there in the center of Half Moon Lick a salt spring flows steadily and to it in droves came the mastodon, and wore out this great depression by their ungainly wallowings in the salty marsh. Dr. Worthen, historian of Illinois, called this spot "the happy hunting ground of the mastodon."

Indians later made salt there and so did white men, since all Gallatin County, in which the Half Moon is located, is underlaid with a brine reservoir.

By 1810 Shawneetown's little furnaces employed 2,000 hands— mostly colored free men, as the law, although permitting slavery then, forbade the use of slaves to work in the salt plants. Orders came in from nearby Kentucky, Indiana, and adjacent territory— more than could be filled by the 100 bushels produced each day. Shipment was mainly by river. The forests yielded fuel.

"The idea never occurred to the salt men," writes Worthen, "that a five-foot seam of coal, through which every one of their wells were dug, could have furnished a never-failing fuel supply right at hand."

The time came when Shawneetown salt reached 100,000 bushels annually. But although located directly on the river it suffered the same fate as Ohio and Kentucky salt; it could not stand up against Kanawha salt coming in increasing great quantities down the river.

In 1850 Shawneetown shut up shop; and although since revived a time or two, all salt making has gone by the board in the half moon where the clumsy mastodon once capered. But before that happened, salt, as you have read, was coming into Illinois from a different point of origin—coming via Chicago and the Lakes and much of it through the agency of Richmond & Comstock, representing the Onondaga salt makers.

And Pennsylvania, too! She made her own salt once upon a time when the nineteenth century was very young. In the valley of the Connemaugh River (which long years afterwards, went on a fierce rampage and destroyed the city of Johnstown) a salt operation of sizeable proportions began about 1813. William Johnson was the man who set it going. He found some water, slightly brackish, oozing up in the fissures of rock near the river, and began boring slowly into the rock near the old town of Loyalhanna. At 45 feet, so says contemporary record, he "struck an abundant fountain strongly impregnated with salt."

Sinking his wooden pipes and setting his fires going under his pans, Johnson was soon making money. His furnace made 30 bushels a day. Following Johnson's lead, other salt-minded men put up their plants. Soon both sides of the unruly Connemaugh blossomed with pumps, kettles, and chimneys.

Then in 1825 something peculiar happened. A man boring at the mouth of Blacklick Creek found, instead of the clear brine he sought, a nasty flow of rather thick, dirty and vile-smelling stuff "of no conceivable use whatever." He gave up in disgust.

Unaware, he had brought in Pennsylvania's first oil well.

With all its furnaces going strong, Western Pennsylvania once reached a high point of 400,000 bushels of salt a year, but in time fell victim to the same malady which had struck the producers of Kentucky and Ohio—that salt from up the Kanawha!

There are salt springs in all parts of the United States. In very few states indeed has no salt at all been produced. The majority of these inland springs have long been forgotten. Some of them made salt commercially, as we have seen, and made it in fairly large quantities.

For all that, at mid-century of the 1800's, we still have the general picture of this Nation's salt supply centered about the three sources mentioned at the beginning of this chapter—Syracuse, Kanawha, and Saltville. Concerning all three, there will be more to say later on.

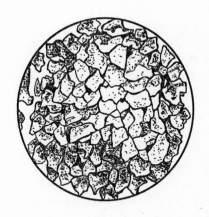

CHAPTER THIRTEEN

. . . AND PASTURES NEW

IN THE SUMMER of 1947 the people of Utah unveiled a majestic monument commemorating the centenary of the founding of their capital, Salt Lake City. The monument stands on a knoll in the lower end of a canyon in the Wasatch Mountains. There, a century earlier (while the United States was yet at war with Mexico) stood Brigham Young, the great Mormon leader, later Utah's first governor, and announced to the band of pioneers who had followed him across the desolate mid-continent stretch of America, the end of their hegira.

"This is the Place!" he said with conviction.

The great valley lay spread out before him. Behind him, the Wasatch Mountains rose impressively, extending in a crescent to the northwest with flat country reaching on beyond to the shores of a salt lake that lay twenty miles to the west, sparkling in the summer sunlight. Brigham Young already knew about that lake. His emissaries had brought him word of its intense salinity.

And less than a month after their arrival, the Mormons turned for salt to the waters of Great Salt Lake.

War with Mexico and the cross-country migration of a persecuted religious sect—these two factors opened up to the Nation yet another vast potential salt cache in the heart of America's then unexplored wastelands. For months President James Polk from the White House in Washington had kept an anxious eye not only on progress reports of Scott's and Taylor's armies in Mexico, but on the marchings of the Mormons. They were on their long trek from Nauvoo, their former capital on the eastern bank of the Mississippi River in Illinois, to find a place where they might establish a colony and live in peace. Would those Mormons, harassed as they had been in New York State, in Missouri, in Illinois, remain loyal to the United States or would they throw in their lot with Mexico?

President Polk, as it shortly turned out, need not have worried. All the Mormons wanted was a place where they could live and work "without let or hindrance." By the terms of the treaty, signed when the war ended, Mexico ceded Utah, along with other wide areas, to the United States. From a small beginning, Utah grew into one of the 48 sovereign states, having a spacious well-built capital city of 165,000, and a flourishing modern salt industry on the shores of the inland sea which Brigham Young had tasted for the first time on a summer day more than a century ago.

If you stand in Temple Square in Salt Lake City today and look west out North Temple Street, you can see dimly—provided the day is clear—the bright waters of Great Salt Lake and rocky Antelope Island rising from its bosom. With the aid of some strong binoculars you would be able to see the gaunt buildings of an extensive salt plant near the lake shore which yields its annual salt harvest of some 100,000 tons to supply not only Utah, but adjacent states as well.

Utah's Great Salt Lake—roughly 80 miles long and irregularly 20 miles wide—carries in its concentrated waters the salty residue of a vastly larger body, ancient Lake Bonneville, which rolled over a mighty region. It was as big as Lake Michigan. Some 25,000 years ago, according to accredited scientists, Lake Bonneville covered much of Utah, spilled over into Montana and Nevada;

filled up numerous depressions and declivities between the Oquirrh (pronounce it "Okwur") and Wasatch Mountains. As proof, the geologists point to high-water marks visible from the center of Salt Lake City on the rugged sides of those hills. So deep was old Lake Bonneville that it would have submerged the tallest building in town and the tallest spire on the Mormon Temple from which the gilt figure of the angel Moroni broods forever over the city of his chosen people.

For countless ages Lake Bonneville lay deep and undisturbed. Then, due to some unknown cataclysm, it tore a hole through Red Rock Pass and Snake River. The great lake drained away into the Pacific Ocean, leaving behind the small puddle which we know as Great Salt Lake. Being a land-locked body, Great Salt Lake has been receiving additional salt deposits through tributary inflow for thousands of years. That accounts for the intense salinity of its waters—six times saltier than the ocean.

"President Brigham and company returned today from the Salt Lake. They gathered some salt from off the rocks along the shore. It is pure, white, and fine as the best that can be bought in the market." So enthusiastically records one of the Mormon "saints" in her diary, as of July, 1847, a fortnight after their arrival in Utah. Yes, the matter of salt very early occupied the Mormons' attention.

A few weeks more and one could see the settlers' iron kettles boiling away on the shore. "The brethren who went down to the lake today to boil salt," continues the Mormon lady diarist, "returned on Monday, August tenth. They report they have found a bed of usable salt ready to load into wagons. It lies between two sand bars and is about six inches thick. They think they can easily load ten wagons without boiling."

They got salt another way, too—by garnering it from the lakeside bushes where salt spray had crystallized. Bringing it into town, they crushed the lumps between stones and made a fairly good, extremely pungent all-purpose salt.

Three years passed, however, before the Mormons realized

that the heat of the Utah summer sun would do their work for them. Once aware of it, they put the sun to good use. Seeing that a light wind would whip up big waves on the lake, they dug trenches behind dikes near the shore. The wind would blow water in waves over into the trenches, thus separating it from the main body. Within a few weeks the sun would evaporate the water in the trench, leaving the salt thick on the bottom. But there was no way of removing the calcium chloride, glauber salts, and other impurities—impurities which partially settle out in the boiling process. When the railroads came in 1869, the Mormons tried ordering salt from the newly opened field in Michigan. The long, long railroad haul, however, entailed enormous transportation charges and that, in turn, shot up the price of the salt. In a short time, more vigorous attempts were made at home production—the beginning of Utah's salt industry.

Judge Elias Smith, one of the venerable residents of Salt Lake City, looks back over eighty years to a boyhood spent in the early days of the colony, and recalls how he made salt.

"It was in the 1860's when I was under twelve years old," Judge Smith says. "With my three brothers I used to work at the salt crusher for fifty cents a day. They would haul the salt in from the lake after they gathered it in the trenches—hard, lumpy, containing all its original impurities. We refined it the only way we then knew how—by dumping it in a big hopper which let it drop down in a steady stream through two rollers that looked more like a big clothes wringer than anything else. One boy on each end of the grinder furnished the horse power.

"No, I can't recall how much we made in a day. It was pretty hard work. But I know this was the first commercial salt making on Great Salt Lake and that we produced enough to supply not only our own community but neighboring towns as well. We'd ship the salt by covered wagons."

The Mormons tell a good and salty yarn concerning the "siege" of Salt Lake City by that body of troops known to them as "Colonel Johnston's Army." It occurred in 1856 when the

Federal Government, hearing rumors of an impending Mormon uprising, sent a force of infantry, cavalry, and dragoons to straighten matters out. Nary a shot was fired, although the Mormons were all set to burn their homes and move out, should there be an attack. Instead, Brigham Young, hearing that the "invaders" were short on rations, especially salt, sent over a wagonload of the Great Salt Lake product to the commanding officer. It was a conciliatory gesture; but Colonel Johnston, a stickler for military etiquette, refused loftily to have any "dealings with the rebels. . . ."

"Alas!" comments the local historian, Stenhouse, "how mutable are human affairs! Five years later that same Colonel Johnston had himself become a 'Rebel'."

He was none other than the famous Albert Sydney Johnston, full general in the Confederate States Army, whose death at the battle of Shiloh eight years later, some historians claim, lost that engagement for the South.

But the salt seems, after all, to have reached the soldiers. The wagoners simply dumped it outside Fort Floyd (where the troops were bivouacked) and drove away. Within a few hours much of the salt had found its way into the military mess.

There'll be more to tell about Great Salt Lake and the way salt is made today.

The Pacific Yields Its Quota

Meanwhile the gold rush of 1849 had brought California zooming into the American consciousness with a loud Western whoop. Back in Chicago, every prospector's wagon, loading up to hit the overland trail, was taking on an ample supply of salt, much of it purchased from Richmond & Company, agents for the Onondaga Salt Association of Syracuse, N. Y. Demand for salt in the Windy City, then a village of twenty thousand, skyrocketed. Not all who went to California, however, went to dig gold. Some enterprising adventurers, knowing that salt was an essential and that the cost of bringing it overland by wagon, or around Cape Horn by ship, was too costly to be practicable, turned to the Pacific Coast waters for a close-at-hand source of supply.

That, however, was not California's first effort. As early as 1770, one year after the founding of California's first white settlement at San Diego, a vessel loaded with Pacific salt sailed away to some unknown port. Five years later Monterey was shipping salt, too. But even so, for many years California salt making remained a haphazard, individual, and sporadic thing. The firm of McCullough, Hartnell & Co. appears to have been the first West Coast commercial salt producer. This company's plant, going full tilt in 1824, seems not to have been especially profitable, for Duflor de Mofras, a world traveler visiting California in 1841, marvels that "despite the rich salt deposits found on the California coast, *ships prefer to bring out their own salt from Boston.*" (It was sold mainly for salting hides.) "Regardless of the long sea voyages, salt from the East has proved relatively cheaper than purchasing local salt, since labor is terrifically scarce."

By 1868, while the gold rush was yet on, eighteen companies had set up their solar plants on the eastern shores of San Francisco Bay. John Barton's mill in Alameda County, where he refined the rough sea product by grinding it, was the largest plant. Less than twenty years afterwards the salt fields were strung out for twenty miles along the shores of the Bay—from Russell Station to Newark, with a score of separate companies on the job. A contemporary newspaper description of the salt making process is enlightening.

"The works consist of a long series of ponds, each an acre in extent. They are separated by levees ten feet high. The whole business resembles a lawn tennis ground done on an immense scale. The square ponds are laid out in sets of seven—that being 'a field'.

"By means of a windmill, salt water is pumped into the first pond until it is eight inches deep. It is then allowed to stand from seven to ten days. Then it is drawn into the next pond, and so it goes through five ponds in succession, remaining the same length of time in each.

"The brine that remains thus becomes heavier and heavier all the time by solar evaporation. By means of a salometer the strength of the brine is determined. When it reaches '25 strong' it is run off into the sixth pond, which is known as the 'making pond'. Here the salt crystals are formed perfectly at '29 strong'. The water appears to be dark red, the bittern having all sunk to the bottom.

"In the sixth pond the salt is allowed to stand and dry for a few days. Then workmen (Chinese coolies for the most part, wearing wide wooden shoes) get in and rake the salt into piles. The piles are usually fifty feet long. In these piles the salt is allowed to cure for several months, after which it is bagged and goes to market.

"The longer salt is allowed to cure, the better it becomes because of its increased dryness. Many manufacturers allow their salt piles to stand four or five years. Under the action of the sun and rain, a hard cement-like crust forms on the outside and protects the salt within. The piles are known as ricks; scattered over the marshes they look like stacks of snow."

A local newspaper of 1886 has this to say concerning California salt: "The native product is much superior to imported salt. Repeated grindings reduce it to the desired fineness. The bulk of the 35,000-ton annual output is used by butchers (packing houses) and bakers."

California, too, has a salt-making sequel as it serves much of the West today.

Thus, before mid-century of the 1800's, two valuable additions to the salt producing capacity of the United States had been uncovered. Removed half a continent, and a continent, respectively, from the settled portion of the country, Utah and California were then important only in their potentialities.

This is the way Salt Lake City — a great metropolis today — looked when salt was first made in Utah.

CHAPTER FOURTEEN

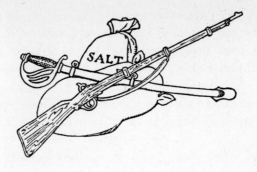

SALT IN AMERICAN WARFARE

AN EX-CONFEDERATE OFFICER, lecturing in Syracuse, New York, one evening shortly after the close of the then late war, made a startling statement. He had been praising the city's extensive salt works.

"Do you know," he asked jovially, "why you Yankees licked us Rebels?...Because you had salt!"

An exaggeration probably, but an exaggeration in the right direction. In all warfare, as Napoleon bitterly observed after his disastrous Moscow campaign, salt is a without-which-nothing in a soldier's wartime diet.

The tremendous exertion of marching and fighting causes the salt content of the human body to drain away in sweat more rapidly than under normal living conditions. Hence, all fighting men must have extra rations of salt to replace the loss. Cavalry horses also must be fed more salt. Salting beef and pork takes a lot more. Tanning harness and leather for artillery and cavalry requires huge quantities of it. It is used in the manufacture of ammunition.

Then, too, civilians of any embattled nation must continue to have their salt quota, if that nation is to survive. A people without, or with insufficient salt becomes a weak people, its citizens frail and lacking in stamina. Bodies in time show the absence of the all-important hydrochloric acid in the gastric juice, due to a lack of sodium-chloride in the blood. And because of that, digestion is hampered; there is a definite tendency toward anemia.

Moreover, when there is no salt to season food, people in disgust join with the patriarch Job in exclaiming: "Can anything unsavory be eaten without salt?"

The ex-Confederate officer at Syracuse told of instances where the lack of salt was hellish, to put it mildly. There was the time Jeb Stuart's cavalry captured those oysters!

It happened at the second Battle of Mananas—sometimes called Bull Run. Hungry, jaded, and saddle sore, the victorious Southerners found among the stacks of other captured supplies many fresh oysters, iced in barrels, the property of the Yankee high-command. Unheard-of delicacies they were to the starved men in grey! They pounced on them with shouts of joy. Under normal circumstances, those bivalves would have lasted about ten minutes. But—

They had no salt!...So, after taking a few half-heartedly, the victors turned away sickened, leaving the bulk of their haul behind.

He knew, also, this Southern soldier, about how the bony cavalry nags of Lee's army developed a fierce, irritating tongue-and-mouth disease, traceable to the absence of salt in their forage. Official tables show that Southerners customarily consume more salt per person than Northerners. Secession officials in Richmond, knowing this, endeavored even in the darkest days of the ill-starred Confederacy, when a soldier's daily ration was reduced to a handful of parched corn and a rind of rancid bacon, to see that each soldier got an ounce or two of salt whenever it was humanly possible. Often, however, even that could not be managed. In fact, the lack of salt posed an insuperable obstacle to Southern resistance.

What is true of the Civil War is true of other American conflicts. Salt played a vital role in all. We have seen to what lengths the American Colonists went to get salt in the War for Independence. By the time the War of 1812 came along, new inland sources of supply had been developed at Syracuse and in the Kanawha Valley.

During those war years (1812-1815) Syracuse produced only 264,000 bushels annually, while Kanawha turned out 600,000 bushels per year.

Thirty years later, however, when we fought the Mexicans, both Kanawha and Syracuse sent salt by ship down the coast, and by steamboat down the Mississippi River, to supply the armies of Scott and Taylor; and Syracuse turned out a million more bushels than Kanawha.

Returning, now, to the officer lecturing in Syracuse; something plausible could be built upon his statement that lack of salt determined the South's fall. Surrender came shortly after its last certain supply of salt was cut off. Salt sold for $1.00 a pound in Vicksburg. Mark Twain tells of seeing a pile of sacked salt on the New Orleans levee in the spring of 1861. One evening, it was worth a couple of dollars a sack; the next morning, its weight in gold, to such dizzy heights had the war sent the price of this commonplace article.

"It is only when a prime necessity thrusts itself upon public attention by its absence that a person ceases to take it for granted," remarks Ella C. Lonn, in her admirable book, *Salt as a Factor in the Confederacy*. "Only when he no longer has it, does he realize what an important ingredient for his palate and digestion is plain ordinary salt, necessary alike to man and beast."

The North had no salt problem. Syracuse made enough both for Federal armies and civilians. The high point of Onondaga production, indeed, came during the war years. Better still, the North had the means to transport and distribute it.

Monument in salt — Wieliczka mine, Poland.

Chapel in a Salt Mine, Wieliczka, Poland.

Here you see an old salt boat passing through the weigh-lock on the Erie Canal, Syracuse, before the Civil War.

Joy Morton was a key figure in the American Salt Industry.

Joseph M. Duncan adapted the vacuum pan to salt making.

Storm coming in Syracuse! Hurry and Cover the Salt Vats! 1855.

(Courtesy, Crandall Melvin, president, Merchants Bank.)

The Confederacy's salt experience, on the other hand, forms part of our national salt epic. Its entire four-year life was one relentless struggle to get salt and to distribute it to the places where it was needed—to armies and civilians alike. Not only was the salt supply scarce but the South's railroad network as of 1860 reached only a fractional part of a vast territory. Highways were dirt roads, impassable during a good part of the year; and one by one, as these highways and the rail lines fell into Northern hands they became useless to the Confederates.

A black market in salt flourished throughout the Confederacy's four-year life, aggravating the shortage.

Along the Atlantic coast lay the watchful ships of Lincoln's blockade, effectively shutting off salt imports. It was a time for rejoicing when a single wily blockade runner could slip in with a cargo of salt. As a result of the blockade the Mississippi and Ohio River system had, by the end of 1862, become well-nigh useless for transporting salt. The Yankees held the rivers, too.

"Hold the Kanawha salt works in Western Virginia!" President Jefferson Davis orders Lee in 1861. So a Grey army under General Wise moves west from Richmond, across the Alleghanies, down into the Kanawha Valley. Spang in the middle of the valley, it meets a strong Federal force moving up from Ohio, on both sides of the Kanawha River, the commander, General Jake Cox, riding upstream and directing the attack from the pilot house of the steamboat. The shots ring out; the field guns bark; the Grey forces fall back.* The salt works pass to Northern hands. Off goes a long wagon train carrying salt to Northern encampments, after which Cox's men systematically destroy the furnaces, knock down the pumps, fill in the wells.

But the South tries again. The following year comes General Loring's Confederate brigade and drives out Cox's men. Once

---

*Among the military companies which marched out with Wise, was the Kanawha Riflemen, made up of the valley's best young bloods—many, scions of salt-making families. Commander of this crack company was a young graduate of Virginia Military Institute, named George S. Patton. As a Colonel, he was killed in the battle of Winchester in 1864. His grandson, George S. Patton III became famous in a later war.

more the South holds the Kanawha salt fields and more than a quarter-million bushels, made at the repaired furnaces, moves out to salt-hungry secessionists.

The end was not yet. Loring's men in turn were driven out late in 1862 by an invading army under General Lightburn, and for the last time Kanawha changed hands. The Confederacy had to look elsewhere for salt because, within a few months, all that part of Virginia west of the Alleghanies, including Kanawha, became a new and separate state of the Union, West Virginia, no longer part of the Confederacy.

Loss of Kanawha left only one important salt-producing center within Southern boundaries. That was Saltville, high in the Alleghany Mountains. Saltville's history for the next two and a half years was one of intense activity. Where in pre-Revolutionary times, Charles Campbell and other pioneers boiled natural brine under the tutelage of Mary Ingles, fresh back from her Indian captivity, big furnaces with hundreds of kettles redoubled their output. Saltville's job was to supply as many of the far-flung seceded states as possible. Each of these individual commonwealths sent up its force of workmen to make salt for its own separate needs. From all directions came heavy wagons, by the thousands, literally, to haul back the precious white grains to distant states.

Meanwhile a force of Grey cavalry and infantry guarded the salt furnaces. Then too, the salt-makers themselves doubled in brass; they were trained to run out at a moment's notice, pick up their rifles and from the trenches on the hillside fire down on the invaders.

Three times during the war the North sent an attacking force to knock Saltville into a cocked hat. Three times the North failed. John Morgan's cavalry beat them off once; Breckenridge's men another time; McCausland's cavalry yet another. But at long last, late in 1864, a few months before Lee's surrender, came a strong attacking force marching in through Saltville's little amphitheatre of surrounding hills that look like shapely haystacks. The attacking general placed two regiments of Negro troops in front to bear the brunt. Rebel rifles spat viciously down from the hillside. But it was no use—Saltville fell. The furnaces were broken, the wells filled in with scrap iron. The last of the South's important salt centers was gone.

But something significant had meanwhile occurred in the far South—something which was in time to augment the entire American salt supply. More than a year before Saltville fell, rock salt was found in southern Louisiana. Near the historic old town of New Iberia (it's in the Evangeline country, the home of the descendants of the expatriated French Canadians) there is a piece of land extending into the Gulf of Mexico known as Avery Island. At one time it was an island in fact, but had become joined to the mainland. Early settlers in 1791 found springs on this island having a brine strong enough to yield salt for local use.

Later, Old Hickory Jackson's army, fighting the Battle of New Orleans after the end of the War of 1812, got its quota of salt from the brine on the island. Still later, during the Civil War, one of Judge Avery's Negroes was deepening a salt spring in order to get stronger brine and had dug down sixteen feet. His shovel suddenly struck what seemed to be a big rock.

"Tain't no use, Mister John," he called up to Judge Avery's son who was bossing the job. "Can't git down no deeper. Done hit a rock." It was a rock indeed, but a later examination showed it to be a rock of pure halite.

To the salt-starved South this discovery seemed manna from Heaven. The French geologist, Thomassy, came over from New Orleans and examined the mine, and said there was enough salt to supply the entire Confederacy for forty years or more. Which was all very fine, had there been any way to ship and distribute it generally. But rivers and sea lanes were cut off; there were no adjacent railroad lines; a wagon haul of more than a thousand miles was necessary to reach Lee's struggling Virginia forces. These hard facts faced the rebellious South.

For all that, Judge Avery was besieged by state government and civilians alike. They all wanted salt contracts. For a time Louisiana and Texas non-combatants, and nearby armies, received great benefits from the salt mines—mines which are worked extensively and profitably to this day. Later General Banks led a mighty expedition against the Avery Island salt mine and captured it for the Federals.

Nature has put plenty of rock salt along the entire Gulf Coast in both Louisiana and Texas. It lies in subterranean blocks known as "domes." That means simply that the salt strata long ago were pushed up at various places—probably by volcanic action—within the earth. The humps or domes, so pushed up, as some points extend above the surface of the water or of level land surrounding them. Salt mines are now sunk into the tops of the domes and from the vertical shaft rooms or entries are run out laterally in different directions. From these the salt is mined, and hoisted to the surface.

The South resorted to every conceivable expedient to get salt. Nearly every Southern state had its salt licks and springs though not many could be worked profitably. The war, however, drove many a planter and farmer to work the springs on their own lands for their own use. The State of Alabama took over and worked many of its own springs, and wagons from nearby states came to take away what they could get.

Next, the dried-up salt lakes or ponds in the vicinity of El Paso, Texas, were called upon to yield their meed of the seasoner. These "dry lakes" were puddle remainders of the old Permian Sea which ages ago lay over this region. For many years Mexicans came there to get salt. The Confederacy, in its need, built a road over the sands and sent its wagons at the end of the rainy season to scrape up the one-inch layer of salt from the dry lake beds.

Around these same ponds clings a bloody memory of an incident involved in the question of who owned them. It happened not so long after the Civil War; the Texas Rangers were involved in it. Texans call it their "Salt War." . . . But that's another story.

As men have done from time out of mind, the Confederates also turned to the ocean for salt. Dozens of little inlets, bays and bayous along the Florida and Carolina coasts came alive with smoking, busy furnaces. There the sea brine was boiled

An artist's idea of how Federal naval forces attacked and destroyed a Rebel seacoast salt "factory."

and caches of salt were stored. So desperate was the South's need that Richmond offered immunity from military service to all men who would work the kettles. There seems to have been no lack of volunteers to do the work! Screened behind the semi-tropical foliage, some of these furnaces made as much as 1,800 bushels a day.

The Federal naval expeditions, fitted out to destroy these solar plants, and the difficulties they met with, make an interesting and little-known chapter of naval history. Due to the iron shortage, the coast plants found that by taking old harbor buoys and sawing them in half, they had very good kettles of 150 gallons each.

In some isolated sections of the South, people were reduced to the expedient of digging out earth from underneath smokehouses and boiling it to get what salt they could. And, among the first things the hungry Grey soldiers asked for, following the surrender, was a generous helping of the good old sodium chloride, without which "food ain't worth eating."

Here on Avery Island is where Rock Salt was first discovered in the United States.

PART TWO

THE OLD ORDER CHANGETH...

CHAPTER FIFTEEN

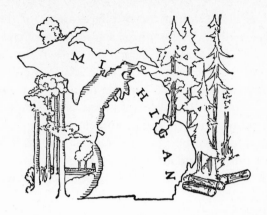

THE OLD ORDER CHANGETH . . .

A SEVERE HURRICANE hit Syracuse, New York, in the 1920's and helped do a job already under way—that of demolishing the last of the salt plants. It was the old far-spreading solar works of Thomas Gale, a name which had been associated with salt making since 1840. When the storm died down, all that remained of a wide area of sheds, pumps, vats, and reservoirs, were acres of rotting timber and twisted, rusty machinery.

Thus ended an era. Onondaga salt making, declining through many years, succumbed finally after a lingering illness which may be summed up in the phrase "competition from other and newer sources." The Erie Canal, too—that highway which salt had built and over which so large a part of Onondaga's total output moved to market—had likewise fallen upon evil days. It was being filled in to make a surfaced highway, though the New York State Barge Canal, its successor, much larger and deeper, is doing a large business today.

Presently we shall look at the specific reasons for the demise of so lush a growth as the Onondaga salt industry. First, though, what about the city, Syracuse, which had grown up out of the muck and brine on the shores of the little lake? America's inland cities evolved from any one of a number of causes or combination of causes. Syracuse, as we have seen, was born simply because of a single industry which began and flourished there in the wilderness. Salt created her, fostered her, nourished her; so that she grew up into a maiden of stately proportions, laving her white feet in the natural brine which bubbled up within her gates.

Making the kettles, pipe, and machinery for the salt plants gave Syracuse her start along industrial lines. Thus when salt making came to a halt, the city went right along manufacturing other things. Fifth in the list of New York State's galaxy of cities (population 230,000), Syracuse makes refrigerators, typewriters, motor cars, shoes, and a lot of other things which her chamber of commerce will be glad to tell you about.

Moreover, Solvay and other chemical plants have located in Syracuse to utilize the brine made from the deep-lying rock salt beds and brought up by modern drilling and pumping.

The gentlemen at the Chamber, however, are known to get hot under the collar when they see in books and magazines pictures of modern Syracuse with salt boats on the Erie Canal tied up at Clinton Square. Such pictured anachronisms have actually been known to appear in very recent years!

This fact remains, for all that: it was the imperative national need for her salt that overcame the early natural disadvantages of Syracuse's location—since made pleasant and convenient. Salt drew to her doors the first big highway of transport. Salt, as mentioned, bred the beginning of her subsequent importance and the name "Salt City" is likely to cling to her for a long time to come. Walking through the city you see the name Cooper Street. That was once a lane on which were numerous shops that made the barrels for the salt. The name Salina, of course, on her main thoroughfare, memorializes forever not only her early name but the sodium chloride from which she took her first name.

Though thoroughly metropolitan now, Syracuse remembers the wild gusto of life in the old days. For salt making was a rough business. It bred a race of men that, for toughness, would stand up rather well beside the roistering flatboatmen of old Mississippi River. Before Salina and South Salina had been joined under the name of Syracuse, as told in another chapter, fierce riots frequently took place between the rival salt boilers of the two towns. They organized armies and they fought for pleasure.

In the Forties occurred the memorable clash between the Salina "Invincibles" and the Syracuse "Sluggers." Both factions became heavily lickered up, fought with stones, shillalahs, and knives; and a number of broken heads resulted. Division Street, the no-man's-land between the two communities, marks today the place where the opposing scrappers put up barricades of overturned horsecarts and milk carts and "fit it out" to the finish.

Then there was the Coffee House riot. That happened in the Forties, also, on a New Year's Eve. Robbery and threatened assault on peaceful citizens caused the Mayor to call out the local military company, Captain Teall's Cadets, to restore order. As the leaders of the two armies were carried to the clink, they were heard to growl: "We're going down to Albany where we can fight in some peace."

It was to prevent such clashes between two antagonistic salt towns that they were united under the name of Syracuse. Had it not been for salt, there might still have been two towns where one now grows and prospers.

Aiming at a Better Product

"An Act to improve the Quality of Salt Manufactured in the County of Onondaga." So ran the title of a law passed in Albany in 1850. Complaints had been coming in for a long time—well founded complaints. At first, apparently nobody expected a good, clean salt. Salt was salt, wet or dry, soiled or clean. But as time went on, the public became more discriminating.

"The salt is dirty." "It cakes up in dry weather." "It's damp." So ran the complaints.

For the first time, therefore, the state asked chemists to test the brine. The chemists reported, "If you will apply scientific methods to making salt, you will get a better product."

"The job is yours," New York State Salt Superintendent Robert Gere told the eminent scientist, Dr. George H. Cook.

After months of experimenting, Dr. Cook announced that he had tried putting lime in the boiling brine. That clarified it but left the salt even damper than before. A little lime also got into the finished product, which was not good.

"Try alum," the doctor recommended. "It precipitates the oxide of iron most effectually. The expense is trifling; two pounds of alum will take care of 5,000 gallons of brine."

The salt makers made a thorough trial and declared that alum actually did the work. It got rid of the reddish cast which had resulted in ugly salt, left a clean, white product which dried in a short time.

And just about this time came an early experimenter suggesting a novel method of manufacture. He was S. B. Howd and he was some years ahead of his time.

"To precipitate impurities fully," Howd reported, "I heat my brine in closed vessels to a temperature of 280 degrees. Then I force it through pipes into another closed vessel or boiler where saturation takes place, and finally into open pans or vats, aided by steam."

*   *   *   *

Now for the reasons responsible for Onondaga's eclipse and decline. The panic of 1857 played hob with many of the salt makers in Syracuse. They had to fold up and go out of business. Nevertheless, the industry during the ensuing eight years rose to the peak of its production. That was during the War of the

States, when the emergency called for every pound of salt that could be made. Trouble lay ahead, however; trouble in the guise of increasing competition. First there was the importation of foreign salt, following the end of the war. Then, Kanawha salt, now that the canal from Lake Erie to the Ohio River was open, and rail lines extended, began to encroach further on Onondaga territory. A new salt field had been opened in Pomeroy Bend on the Ohio River, working with a brine that was stronger even than Kanawha's. These were all contributory to the fall of Syracuse supremacy. And then, still another salt field flung open its gates—Michigan.

Natural brine had been discovered at Saginaw, Michigan, late in the 1850's, and salt making began there in a small way during the Civil War. In the bitter competition of those days for the cream of the trade, Michigan salt men began an intensive advertising campaign, proclaiming loudly that their salt was cleaner, drier, and purer than that of either Kanawha or Syracuse. They made no bones about advising their prospective patrons to throw the Easterners overboard and buy from Michigan. The first deep salt well in Michigan, at St. Clair, was sunk by a man named Thompson. And very soon Michigan salt was on the market.

Yes, Michigan presented a threat to Syracuse's western trade. Michigan's brine was really stronger. The Onondaga product had been distributed in Chicago and through the entire West by the Chicago salt agency. You will recall that Alonzo Richmond, sent out by the Onondaga Salt Association in 1848, had established this agency. It was destined for big things. But Michigan being nearer Chicago and the West than Syracuse, the extra cost in transporting Onondaga salt placed handicap on the latter. You simply can't furnish a cheap commodity, however great the demand, at a price to compete with the same commodity produced closer to the point of consumption.

Another thing: the meat industry had come into being in Chicago (see another chapter) just following the end of the war. Orders for enormous quantities of salt which Armour,

Swift, and other packers needed for curing meat, all went to the Chicago agents. This new big market was entirely shut off from Onondaga by the long freight haul which intervened.

And yet another factor eventually contributed to the death of the Syracuse salt industry. In two or three decades following the end of the Civil War, a veritable salt craze hit other New York counties with a bang. Seeing the success of Onondaga, these new prospectors sank wells in many parts of the state—little plants, for the most part, springing up overnight, each competing with the other for the trade which could not consume the output of all. In short, there were too many cooks in the business and they spoiled the brine. Still, during the years they flourished, these mushroom plants took just that much from the business which Syracuse was enjoying.

And so Onondaga began to slip. The decline was slow, through the 'Seventies, 'Eighties, 'Nineties, and well into the twentieth century, each succeeding year showing a dwindling total output. It was toward the end of the century, seeing that the business was on the skids, that the State of New York released its control over the Onondaga industry. But even under complete private control the decline continued.

The hurricane, as recorded, finished the job.

And What About Kanawha?

Kanawha was having its troubles, too. Had you asked Dr. Hale, head of the Kanawha salt trust in the 1870's, what the outlook was for the salt business in the Kanawha Valley, he would have said, "There's enough brine still under the State of West Virginia to supply the whole United States with salt for years to come."

And probably he would have been right in his statement. But he wouldn't have taken into account, in such an estimate, the cost of hauling salt to market. Kanawha's market at that time was apparently sure. Cincinnati was the national meat-packing center—Kanawha's best customer. It was not possible to foresee in 1870 that Chicago's new meat-packing industry would in time supplant Cincinnati's, thereby cutting the latter's demand for salt almost to the vanishing point. Nor did they foresee that the new salt field at Pomeroy was big enough to worry about.

But these things actually came about. The meat-packing industry took a long westward leap from Cincinnati to Chicago. Salt wells began to dot the Ohio's shore near Pomeroy.

Pomeroy is a town 100 yards wide and five miles long. It consists mainly of a long thoroughfare paralleling the river, and many pretty homes scattered about on the terraced hills that rise precipitately from the river bank. So close are the hills to the river that salt men in Pomeroy get their fuel from coal mines in their own back yards. The Pomeroy family, for whom the town is named, began making salt in 1850. An employee of the Pomeroy family sank a well and established his own furnace in 1859. That plant exists and produces today—the last active operation of twenty-six salt furnaces that once turned out enough salt to become a major factor in the blotting out of Kanawha.

They still talk in Pomeroy of the time when a big sidewheel steamboat the *Bonanza* nosed out from the city wharf with 3,600 barrels of salt on board. Her decks ran nearly awash and it is a wonder that she reached Cincinnati without mishap. It was Pomeroy's proximity to Cincinnati (she's many miles nearer than Kanawha) that gave her her start. Moreover, Pomeroy's brine is a little stronger than Kanawha's.

We saw in an earlier chapter how Ohio's early salt-making efforts went on the rocks in the early days of the nineteenth century because it could not compete with Kanawha salt. Well, Ohio had her revenge with the rise of Pomeroy. Kanawha, meanwhile, found her eastern trade deeply cut into by Saltville, Va., following the Civil War. This was another contributory factor to the windup of the second most important of America's salt-producing centers.

Saltville, third of the early "Big Three," in turn suffered also.

Photo Bettmann Archive

As an artist for Harper's Weekly (1864) saw a salt furnace fireman at Saltville, Va.

The long arm of Michigan reached even that highland fastness in Virginia.

Under the pressure of the Civil War, Saltville was making 10,000 bushels a day in 1863. The Holston Salt and Plaster Company took over in 1865. Production had fallen to 3,000 bushels a day by 1887. Six years later Saltville's prestige as a salt producer ended.

This is not to say that any of the original big three—Syracuse, Kanawha, or Saltville—suffered from a shortage of brine. Nature's supply in the "subterranean lake" beneath both Kanawha and Pomeroy, in the stratification under Syracuse, and in the deep-lying salt beds beneath Saltville seems not to run out. And though salt making as an important industry is a thing of the past, the brine is still put to excellent use.

It was in 1883 that the Semet Solvay Company located the first of its American plants near the spot where Asa Danforth and Comfort Tyler made salt in what is now Syracuse. Solvay is still there, using vast quantities of Onondaga brine to make chemicals.

Saltville has her chemical activity, too; the big plant of the Matheson Alkali Works has succeeded to the place where Mary Ingles first taught Virginia pioneers to make salt on the tract of land settled by Charles Campbell nearly two hundred years ago, and from which the briny lake has been drained.

The Kanawha Valley has also become one of America's most important chemical regions. Companies locate their important operations here because they have only to drill down to assure themselves of an endless supply of brine to use in their manufacturing processes.

The Erie Canal at Syracuse prior to 1860

CHAPTER SIXTEEN

THE NAME MORTON COMES INTO
THE SALT BUSINESS

TWO MEN MET in a room above a store in Aurora, Illinois, on a Sunday afternoon in 1879. One was past middle age and looked it. The other was young, tall, vigorous, brown-eyed, and had about him a look of latent power.

"So you are Joy Morton," said the older man pleasantly as they shook hands. "Your brother Paul told me about you, Mr. Morton. My name is Wheeler."

The younger man smiled. "I hope he said nice things, Mr. Wheeler. Have a seat, sir."

"Oh, yes, he did! And that's one reason why I'm here. I ought to explain that I come in contact with your brother frequently. Being a salt broker in Chicago, I ship considerable by the Burlington Railroad, of which he's the Chicago freight agent. I was telling him a few days ago that I need a young man with some capital to come in with me on a partnership basis. He suggested you at once."

He paused for a moment, while Morton waited. Presently he went on:

"Do you like your work here in Aurora?"

"Yes," the other replied after a moment's thought. "Being a storekeeper for the Burlington Railroad is all right. There's promotion ahead. But naturally I've always hoped some day to be in business for myself—not a hired man. I have a little capital."

Mr. Wheeler nodded. "I see. Well, let me give you a brief outline of our company's background and the scope of its business. You can better decide, after that, whether it interests you."

"I'd like to hear it."

The little salt agency which he headed, Mr. Wheeler explained, was an old one—as age was reckoned in the young city of Chicago. Thirty-one years earlier, in 1848, young Alonzo Richmond had been sent out by the Onondaga salt men's association to sell New York salt in the West and at once the orders began to roll in.

Chicago, even then, was growing like Jack's beanstalk, spreading out along the lake shore and back over the prairies. Already wagon trains were outfitting in town to strike out across the plains to establish new homes and communities farther west. Only a year following Richmond's arrival, news came that gold had been discovered in California. That, Mr. Wheeler stated, had meant a still greater demand for salt, for prospectors. Canal boats had just begun to run steadily up the Chicago River and through the new Illinois and Michigan Canal to the Mississippi Valley, distributing salt and other cargoes to river markets at much lower rates than had before been possible. Plank roads had been laid over the swamps in and around the city; and every day saw a long procession of farm wagons come rolling into Chicago bringing produce and taking out supplies, not the least important of which was salt. Sometimes these wagons got stuck in the mud on the main thoroughfare of that unpaved Chicago of 1848 and remained there all night while wolves howled and frogs in nearby marshes made night hideous.

Richmond & Company had rung up a profit the very first year of their business. And with each succeeding year—although the agency had changed owners and personnel several times, the firm name being successively Richmond & Comstock; Haskins, Martin & Wheeler; Elkins, Wheeler & Company and now, E. I. Wheeler & Company—they had rolled up larger shipments and increased profits.

Hand in hand with the growth of Chicago—from a sprawling town of one- and two-story frame houses to a handsome, well-built metropolis of five- and six-story buildings and railroads bringing a hundred trains a day—the calls for salt grew steadily, so that now it was moving out of Chicago by both railroad and canal.

Not even the panic of 1857, Mr. Wheeler pointed out, had retarded the salt business, although many another good Chicago firm had gone on the rocks. The demand continued all through the Civil War and following the end of that conflict came Armour, the first of the big meat packers to set up shop in Chicago. Others followed within a few years.

"The packing-house trade has greatly increased the annual business of our agency," the speaker continued. "And it was just about the same time in the Sixties that our source of production suddenly shifted. They found brine and rock salt up in Michigan. That's many miles nearer Chicago than Syracuse, New York, where we'd been getting the Onondaga salt."

Up in Michigan, where logs were being cut and floated by river down to the sawmills, some lumbermen had set up salt blocks of their own, with rows of pans and kettles to evaporate the brine, using wood for fuel. This was a way in which they could use up their continually accumulating pile of forest waste, turn an expense into a profit.

Transportation costs, Mr. Wheeler explained, played a very big part in the retail price of salt. The longer the haul, naturally the higher the delivered price. So, since Michigan could produce salt more cheaply, the agency gave up its Onondaga connection and became agent for Michigan salt. A Michigan Salt Association was established in 1870. From Saginaw, Bay City, St. Clair, Ludington, and Manistee boats could bring salt straight over the Lakes to the docks at Chicago and other lake cities.

The agency's business continued to expand even as the city expanded. It was in 1874 that Wheeler took over the business in partnership with Elkins. Then, on the latter's retirement, the full burden devolved upon Wheeler.

"Now, my health is none too good, and none of the four clerks in my office are executive material," Mr. Wheeler concluded. "At the same time, our business keeps on growing and the responsibilities keep piling up. That's why I need a man to come in with me. I believe this is an excellent opportunity for a young man. Chicago is growing faster than any other American city; it needs young men with vision, with the ability to sell, and to work hard."

Young Morton listened as his caller talked—listened with growing interest. He was turning the offer over in his mind carefully, weighing his present work and opportunity with the work and potential opportunities which would be his if he accepted this offer and moved to Chicago. It was a vital decision to make, not to be snapped at hastily.

"Will you give me a little time to think it over, Mr. Wheeler?" he asked finally.

"Certainly. If you come to see me in Chicago in about a week, that will be perfectly satisfactory. I want you to take your time."

A week later, Morton had another talk with Mr. Wheeler at the latter's Chicago home. The upshot was that he agreed to invest his entire capital of nearly $10,000, saved from wages, and from some wise real estate investments. That bought him a one-fifth partnership in the firm of E. I. Wheeler & Company —he being the "& Company!"

Joy Morton was then twenty-four years old. Born in Detroit, his mother had taken him in his infancy back to the family farm in Nebraska. There he grew up, a pioneer lad in a pioneer land. His father, J. Sterling Morton, was acting territorial governor (Nebraska has no state debt today because he insisted that she do business on a cash basis) and later would be Grover Cleveland's Secretary of Agriculture and the founder of Arbor Day.

As a child, Joy learned to love the outdoors. He also loved traveling back and forth on the little Missouri River steamboats that furnished the chief means of ingress and egress in those days. More than once, as a young man, he'd driven wagons across the plains, and had carried a rod on surveying parties. His first regular job had been with a bank in Nebraska City.

Later he had taken on a railroad job. Then meningitis laid him low for many months. Following that, he regained his health and vigor by managing the family farm, Arbor Lodge, spending most of his time in the open air. Meanwhile, he did some careful investing on the side which paid him well.

The new salt man entered with enthusiasm upon his work. Wheeler had wanted a man to assume the main burden of the business. In his young partner he found what he was looking for—alertness, an eagerness to find out everything about the business, enormous energy and a natural aptitude for bringing in orders. Almost as soon as he had assumed his duties, the new man made his influence felt in salt circles. He studied the markets, production figures, and freight rates. The demand for salt he balanced against the available supply.

And so the years marched on. The time and the place—Chicago in the "elegant Eighties"—combined to create admirable conditions for a young man equipped mentally and physically to head a growing enterprise. It was a young man's town—brisk, a trifle crude, but fast acquiring the sophistication of a great city. Scars of the devastating fire which had struck the city in 1871 had largely been removed. That cataclysm merely made way for a newer and more impressive metropolis, now assuming form. The population was nearly a million and a head start had been made towards a city such as the Midwest had never known.

Such fine structures! The new Board of Trade Building, with its ornate high center tower, spread itself along Jackson Street, facing straight up LaSalle—a thoroughfare developing into a financial center second only to Wall Street in New York. On Michigan Avenue at Adams, Mr. Pullman was putting up a fine new red brick building to house his Palace Car Company. The fire had destroyed his earlier headquarters at Randolph and Michigan.

The big Trade Exhibition Building sprawled on the Lake Shore where the present Art Institute stands. Inside one could see permanent displays of Chicago's manufacturers and merchants—tangible testimony of the city's growing mercantile importance.

Fine homes were going up on the near South Side, replacing the beautiful Terrace Row on Michigan Avenue, destroyed in the fire. The names of Potter Palmer, Levi Leiter, and Marshall Field were becoming increasingly important in State Street retail circles. A young man named Henry Lytton (who, as these words are written, has reached his 101st year and is the dean of State Street merchants) was doing a land-office business in low-priced men's suits on State Street at Jackson. The new cable cars sped along State Street. The fine Palmer House had become a nationally-known hostelry. The elder Carter Harrison was Mayor. Money was plentiful. Business hummed. There were fortunes to be made and many of the young men whose names were beginning to be heard about town were destined to make them.

Among the names you heard in Chicago business circles in those days was that of Morton, the rising young salt broker. Referring to those early Chicago years, Mr. Morton once said: "I left the bulk of my earnings in the business, since I felt that some day we were going to do a lot of expanding. Our territory was steadily increasing, spreading west of the Mississippi River."

With that growth of territory grew the responsibility which Morton found himself called upon to assume. Mr. Wheeler's health did not improve. In the middle Eighties, in quest of restoration, he took a trip overseas. But it was too late. He died in Geneva, Switzerland, in the fall of 1885.

"He was very generous and fair," the junior partner said afterwards. "Our relations were always most pleasant."

Mr. Wheeler's holdings passed to his widow, Morton taking complete charge of the business. Gradually he had increased his share of the capital until he owned a full half interest.

The following year he made a satisfactory arrangement with the Wheeler estate, buying out his late partner's interest for $25,000. Thus, within the short space of seven years, the youth who had come in as a junior partner in the salt brokerage office, found himself the head of that business. He took in with him his brother Mark Morton on a partnership basis, and the name on the Lake Street office window became:

JOY MORTON & COMPANY

The forests of Michigan meanwhile were rapidly thinning out under the heavy encroachments of the lumber industry. It became clear to Morton that the time would come—and not many years hence—when the sawmills which had been furnishing waste wood for fuel to run the salt plants, would cease to supply that fuel. Therefore, he prepared to meet the situation.

He realized that although the forests would be gone in time, the brine and the rock salt would remain. Using another fuel to replace wood, Michigan salt could still be produced and moved to the growing West through Chicago, the natural gateway. Morton pondered these facts and on them made his plans for the future.

A new factor now entered the picture. Salt in Kansas! The Democratic National Committee met in St. Louis in the summer of 1888. Morton invited the members of the Michigan Salt Association, for which he was agent, on a jaunt which, as it turned out, had momentous consequences. After attending the convention sessions and seeing Cleveland safely nominated, the Morton party went on in its private car to Hutchinson, Kansas.

"Excitement was running high in Hutchinson because rock salt had been discovered there beneath the Kansas plains," Mr. Morton said. "As salt men, we were interested in new fields—especially where we had potential competitors. You would have thought a gold mine had been opened! Every Hutchinson man and his brother wanted to begin making salt!"

After looking things over, however, the party returned to Chicago. The Michigan men, primarily lumbermen, went on back up the Lake and Mr. Morton returned to his office on Lake Street. The time was not yet ripe for expansion. But he remembered the Kansas situation. His thoughts probably ran something like this: It won't be long before there will be too many salt makers out there, and the balloon will burst. That field is an excellent one for us, should we ever decide to seek markets in the far west."

Joy Morton had meanwhile built a home in Groveland Park, then a residential district lying between Cottage Grove Avenue and the Lake, about 33rd Street on Chicago's South Side. The land had once been a camp for Confederate prisoners, and before that had been part of Oakenwald, estate of Stephen A. Douglas, Illinois's great Democratic statesman. The "Little Giant" himself lies buried in an adjoining park.

In this house the Morton children spent their childhood within sight of the tower of the old University of Chicago buildings. It was a pleasant location. There were wide grassy plots between the rows of houses; and just beyond the Illinois Central tracks lay the blue Lake. Moreover, it was very convenient for Mr. Morton to walk out every morning and take a suburban train to his office down on Lake Street.

Since his coming to Chicago, Morton had looked forward to the time when he would be a salt producer as well as a salt agent. Already his annual sales were mounting through tens of thousands of barrels and tons. The packing houses of Chicago, Kansas City, and elsewhere took a large share of the output. The remainder went to merchants, farmers, and various other purchasers. Then, as more and more customers developed west of the Mississippi, the high railroad rates on the longer delivery haul from Chicago began to turn the retail dealer toward Kansas.

Salt is a heavy commodity, as noted more than once in this volume, and the cost of transporting it always represents a substantial slice of the selling price. The farther the point of consumption from the producing plant, the higher that price must be. As the states west of the Mississippi grew in population, salt consumption grew by leaps and bounds. Morton soon realized that the new Kansas salt must, sooner or later, replace Michigan whenever and wherever that salt could be laid down more cheaply from Kansas than salt from Michigan.

He well remembered his Kansas trip in 1888 and what he had seen there. In the early Nineties the boom which he had foreseen reached its height. Sixteen salt makers were producing in Hutchinson. Hastily-built small plants they were, for the most part, which had sprung up in and around the town and were producing at a great rate, with both pans and kettles. For a time the new Kansas salt prospectors lined their pockets beautifully. But before long each plant found itself launched upon a career of disastrous cut-throat competition with its neighbors. Then, as a sort of sinister climax, the panic of 1893 swept somberly across the country, putting most of the new plants out of business.

CHAPTER SEVENTEEN

GETTING STARTED IN KANSAS

THE PANIC SUBSIDED. Once again Joy Morton visited Hutchinson, Kansas. This time he bought the bankrupt plant of the Diamond Salt Company and set it going. Shortly afterward he rented a couple of other plants. Served by three railroads, Hutchinson occupied a strategic position for salt production and delivery.

More bad luck! Cow Creek, which flows into the Arkansas River at Hutchinson, went on a rampage in 1894 and inundated a large section of the county. Many of the salt plants, Morton's among them, were forced to shut down. At best, the processes at most of these early Hutchinson operations were of an older, inefficient type; their locations, to say the least, hazardous in that they were exposed to frequent floods.

We usually think of Kansas as the great grain-growing state— the Nation's bread basket. The salt to season and flavor the bread made from Kansas wheat and corn likewise comes in large quantities from the same state. A deep, thick layer of rock salt underlies the terrain in and around Hutchinson.

Back in 1860 one J. G. Tuthill gathered spring water from a salt marsh, since known as Tuthill's marsh, in Republic County, and made salt in small amounts. But earlier than that, plainsmen had utilized the natural salt springs of Kansas at various other places. They would come to a spring to butcher and prepare their buffalo meat for the ensuing winters. Near the town of Raymond, on one of the old cattle trails, cowboys used to dig down four feet, find brine, and make salt for themselves, their cattle and their horses.

At Hutchinson, it was Ben Blanchard who in 1887 discovered the presence of salt. He was drilling for oil and natural gas. Purely by accident, he encountered rock salt. This was an exact reversal of the experience of Kanawha and Pennsylvania salt men who, while boring for salt, came upon oil and/or gas! Blanchard lost no time in spreading the news. Screamed the headlines of the local paper:

GREAT SALT MINES TO BE OPENED IN HUTCHINSON!

It really meant a lot to the people of the West. Kansas folks had been compelled to order their salt from far away Michigan via a Chicago salt agency. No wonder the prospect of production close at home brought joy to local hearts. From Warsaw, N. Y., came Dr. A. Guinlock, veteran salt maker. The first plant was put up in 1888 and was under the management of Frank Vincent. It was, indeed, the only plant in full production when Joy Morton and his group made their initial visit to Kansas in 1888. Very shortly, however, followed the mushrooming of many small plants, as already described.

Morton's next move, in his plan to increase production facilities, was to build a salt plant at Wyandotte, Michigan—a coal-burning plant, the first Michigan operation to use fuel other than wood. The forests were continuing to thin out, the lumber companies which made salt "on the side" were making less of it. Morton retained, however, the agency for Michigan Salt Association.

With the growth of his business, he had found himself faced with yet another problem—where to store his salt. To be able to fill orders on short notice, he must keep a large stock of both bulk and barrel salt on hand. The railroads serving Michigan in those days nearly always suffered from chronic car shortage. During the winter months shipments from up there dropped just about to the vanishing point. Then, too, many of the remaining big sawmills which produced salt shut down for the cold months. By bringing salt in ships over the Lakes to Chicago, Milwaukee, and Sheboygan, the salt men could build up a stock against this demand; for there were usually plenty of empty cars available around these large port cities—which was certainly not the case in the small Michigan towns whence the salt originated.

In order to give his customers better and quicker year-round service, Joy Morton decided to put his salt docks and warehouses in Chicago. Older residents of Chicago will recall the long line of water-rail transfer warehouses which, years ago, lined the banks of the Chicago River near the Lake. A portion of the Illinois Central Railroad's old Pier No. 1 had long served such a purpose and Joy Morton leased it in 1888. Step by step he built on the site a warehouse of his own, better adapted to handling salt. Then, needing more office space, he moved his offices (about the time Chicago was celebrating the great Columbian Exposition of 1893) from Lake Street to the front end of one of these new buildings on the pier. As soon thereafter as practicable, he put up his own new offices close by—so close indeed that old employees recall how moving the office necessitated only a short walk across the roof of an intervening warehouse.

The new office building was the exact replica of a famous and historical Massachusetts structure known as the Boston Town House erected by a maternal ancestor of Morton's in the year 1651. Its architectural descendant in Chicago—quaint, arresting in appearance, and very serviceable—housed the company offices for many years.

Those were busy times on the salt dock at I.C. Pier No. 1! There the salt was received in bulk and barrel by boat from Michigan, for storage and reshipment. Loaded to the gunwales, the Lake boats *John Oades, Marion, Minnie Kelton,* or *Normandie* would nose in alongside the dock. Iron buckets, like overgrown old-fashioned coal scuttles, would be filled by workmen in the boats' holds, hoisted up by steam and dumped into hoppers. Hand carts would trundle the salt along the roof and dump it through hatches on to the warehouse floor below. There, workmen with big shovels proceeded to load it as needed. Part of it went into barrels and sacks, a part was moved to boxcars by wheelbarrows for shipment to users of the bulk product— packing houses, and others. Much salt, then as now, went to packing houses direct from Michigan plants.

Joy Morton erected right there on the dock a mill for refining table and dairy salt.

On either side of a long table stood a line of girl workers, one group folding the various sized pasteboard cartons, shaping each over a stationary square block in front of her; another group gluing it and filling it with scoopfuls of salt from the big bin of refined crystals on the table before her.

On the opposite side of the table another line of girls would be filling the cloth pockets (small sacks). As each pocket was filled, a girl sewed it up and seized another.

Hard by, carpenters hammered away on wooden boxes in which to pack those cartons and barrels. Both packers and carpenters soon developed great speed and dexterity. Old employees of the Morton Salt Company today like to tell of the rivalry there was between the two groups—the box makers trying to keep up with the packers, and vice versa.

R. K. Warren, recently retired, after a long service as Treasurer of the Morton Salt Company, recalls the early salt-packing times on the old salt docks:

"In those days the by-product lumber fellows preferred naturally to sell their salt in barrels. The Michigan Salt Association saw to it that the differential between barrels and bulk was high enough to give a good return for the cooperage stock. You see, all the lumber mills made staves and headings for barrels out of what otherwise would be waste lumber—slabs, short pieces, etc.

"Many times I have seen a Lake ship come in with a cargo of bulk salt in her hold, while lashed in among the barrels of the deck load would be the appropriate amount of staves and headings to make the barrels in which to pack the cargo she carried. Later on, however, it became extremely difficult to get cooperage stock. So we endeavored to induce our customers to buy their salt in burlap or cotton bags. It was pretty slow work until the price of barrels went completely out of sight.

"Pressing salt into blocks for stock feeding purposes came into use around the beginning of World War I—an enormous saver of package material. Very little salt is shipped in barrels today." Sterling Morton, chairman of the Morton Salt Company remembers, from his boyhood, scenes in the old cooper shop.

"Our cooperage shops were located on the docks. A force of skilled coopers, working for the usual $2.25 and $2.50 per day, made salt barrels—made 'em out of ash and gum staves and headings, and elm hoops which came to the shops ready cut. The coopers reduced the assembling of barrels to a minimum of movement.

"They worked at a special type of bench over a floor which had a hole into which a form just the size of a barrel head could be placed. First, the cooper would throw down a form hoop slightly larger than the form. Then he'd pick up an armful of staves and rapidly put them in place in the space between the hoop and the head-form—alternating wide with narrow staves. A good cooper's practiced eye could pick out a stave of just the correct width to complete a barrel—make the staves come out even.

"At this point the barrel looked rather like a half-open daisy. Throwing a cable around the daisy's petals (that is, the spreading staves), the cooper would then pull them together with a winch and fit a second form hoop around the upper end. The barrel was now ready for seasoning; in other words, for heating on top of a round iron stove, fired with coke.

"The barrels would stay there long enough for the heat to set the staves in their new position. Workmen used a champhering knife to put the bevel around the top of the staves. Then they would level it off with a plane. Then they'd go to the crozier. The 'croze', in case you don't know it, is the bevel and groove into which the heads fit. The croziers would make this groove with a special curved plane; later crozing machines were developed.

"Extra hoops were then put on above and below the barrel's bulge, a heavy-geared trusser setting them tight. The hooper next took hold of each barrel and replaced the iron hoops, which are really just forms, with permanent elm hoops, and put in the wooden head.

"I can shut my eyes right now and, from out of the past, catch a whiff of the fragrance of our old-time cooper shop—fresh sawdust, shavings, and chips, with an occasional tang of smoke from the stoves! I think youngsters today miss something by not having a chance to visit so fascinating a place as a cooper shop."

CHAPTER EIGHTEEN

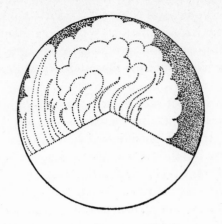

GROWTH, COMPETITION, CONFLAGRATION

THROUGH THE YEARS between the establishment of Joy Morton & Company in 1886 and the turn of the century, American business grew as it had never grown before. In Chicago —that astounding youngster among American metropolises—this growth was such as to make the rest of the country look on with wonder not unmixed with envy.

Figures best tell the tale: Chicago's population in 1880 topped the 500,000 mark. Her manufactures amounted to $250,000,000 annually. Ten years later, 1890, the population had reached a million. But her manufactures, during the same decade, had reached $700,000,000. In other words, Chicago's manufactures almost trebled while the population was doubling.

Such figures could only mean most intense activity for business as a whole in this

> "Town that grows
> Where the Lake wind blows."

The times, of course, were marked by enormous advances in technical and mechanical matters—ways of manufacturing things better; of turning out more products in less time and at lower cost, thus increasing profit for the producer while reducing the price to the consumer.

And as a corollary of such growth we find the words "trusts" and "big business" appearing increasingly in our American language. These terms of possible opprobrium were being used somewhat indiscriminately to apply to almost any two or more large business firms who decided to "jine up" for mutual advantage. The newspapers were full of it! There were beef trusts, and railroad trusts, money trusts, and any number of other kinds of trusts. By the turn of the century, the tendency toward larger business units was in full swing.

Salt, as we have seen in an earlier chapter, set the pace in that direction—Kanawha Valley salt, in fact, way back in the early years of the Nineteenth Century. Then, following the Civil War, salt combinations extended until we find the declining Kanawha activity in league with the venerable Onondaga salt makers, as well as with new and thriving Pomeroy and, for a short time, Michigan salt interests to boot!

These early combinations, which sought to control the salt market and dictate policy, were of greater or less importance; but all were short-lived.

About 1900 there arose a "combine" known as the National Salt Company of New Jersey, which included many salt makers of New York State. Morton was then busy selling, and had just begun to do some salt manufacturing at the new Hutchinson, Kansas, plant. National asked him if he would take over the job of providing warehouse space to store their stock of excess salt.

Vigorous individualist that he was, he preferred to go it alone. He agreed, however, to come in upon his own terms. Those terms were such as left him free to continue his own business and protect him against the blow-up of the "trust," should that ever come about. It *did* come about, as he felt it might, and in a very short time after he had built his warehouses and assembled a mighty stock of salt.

The result, after the tumult and the shouting died, turned out to be very favorable to him. He had turned over his own National Salt Company stock in return for the stock of salt he had stored in his warehouse. Thus, when the National blew up, "he had salt instead of the paper."

But tragedy lay ahead.

No one knew how or where it started—the devastating fire that swept the salt docks and warehouse of Joy Morton & Company in South Chicago on a windy day in 1903. One thing is certain: it did *not* start in the cooper shops where such fires usually have their origin, cluttered as they are with loose staves, shavings, and kiln-dried wood. For the Morton cooper shops remained untouched when the vast warehouse—covering seventeen acres and containing more than 200,000 tons of salt (surely the largest stock ever assembled under a single roof) went up in flames.

Say that a boxcar then carried 25 tons of salt. One can easily estimate the length of the train necessary to haul the stock which Morton had on hand in 1903. It was the dominant factor in the American salt market.

Finally brought under control, the fire left a dark track of desolation. Where had been stacks of good white salt, piled like serried ranges of little hills and protected by roof and walls from the weather, there remained only blackened heaps covered with charred wood. Gaping holes showed where the posts had burned through the salt pile. The heat hardened and solidified the outside of that pile. Where had been a stack of barrel salt, the wood staves and heads were burned away, leaving hard salt cylinders heaped one upon another and covered plentifully with charcoal.

It was not a total loss, however. After the insurance adjustments had been made, workmen were started on the colossal salvage job. The barrel salt was virtually worthless; but it was found by removing a foot or two of the hard outer covering of the bulk piles that clean salt lay underneath. So machines got to work and for years the "mining" went on. Even that portion of the salvage which was plentifully sprinkled with charred wood was not lost. Charcoal, as any sensible farmer can tell you, is an excellent ingredient for stock food; therefore Morton's "charcoal blend" received a ready welcome by farmers. In the course of time, the entire stock of the remaining bulk salt was disposed of.

Fires and cave-ins (or, as scientists call them, land subsidences) rank first among the hazards which formerly plagued American salt makers. The fires resulted from the amount of wood necessarily used in the great sprawling refinery and warehouse structures. The cave-ins followed when the taking out of salt at places where it occurs fairly close to the surface of the ground left large hollow places. The surface simply sank (subsided) into the hole.

Morton was to experience, inevitably, his share of both. But he profited by each experience in that the succeeding plants which he built were of much sturdier construction, having greater fire resistance, and that modern scientific methods were applied to sinking wells and mines to tap underground salt deposits.

The big South Chicago fire of 1903 indeed was not his first at that place. There had been an earlier fire in 1897, also at South Chicago. Its results, however, were not so devastating as the conflagration of 1903.

Undaunted by the second fire, Morton rebuilt in part his South Chicago warehouse. Then, in order not to have his entire stock under one roof, he put up a new warehouse in the city proper, on the Burlington Railroad docks at Hoyne Avenue, just south of Blue Island. Former Dock Manager, John R. Cooper, now retired, recalls how the new docks worked.

"We moved lots of salt from South Chicago after the big fire and stored it in these new Burlington docks. Our old lake

schooner *Frank C. Leighton* did the job for us, making one
trip after another. Those were big warehouses. That in which
we stored our bulk salt had a capacity of more than 40,000 tons,
and we kept it full. It was about 250 feet long and there were
three bays of gabled roof construction. We used to stack our
salt in mountains 40 feet high—a lot too high, as we know now,
for safety.

"How did we handle it? We had an overhead trolley on
which a big one-ton bucket ran by gravity. Very efficient, though
sometimes the cable would break in the course of the day's work,
and shoot the whole blamed business down the length of the
track, out through the wall of the building, over the railroad,
to wind up within a couple of feet of McCormick's foundry!

"Yes, those were exciting days. Luckily we had no fatalities.
And when you think of it, it's a wonder we never hit anybody.
You can imagine what a sweet job it was after such an accident
to get that pile of junk untangled, hoist it up 40 feet, and set
her going again.

"We had a very nice steel shed to store our barrel salt in.
But it could accommodate only 20,000 barrels, and we made it
a rule to carry a stock of from 40,000 to 50,000 barrels on hand.
So we had to store the rest of it out on the prairie under a tem-
porary board roof. We have learned a whole lot better since
those days! After a few months out there in the weather, we'd
scrape away the snow to get at the lower tier of barrels and find
them mashed down and flattened out so that they looked more
like boxes than barrels. You couldn't roll them if you had to!"

Very early in the new century another combination of salt
makers came into being to replace the defunct and unlamented
National Salt Company. This was a much more stable and (from
the customer's as well as the manufacturer's viewpoint) more
dependable and satisfactory organization. It was known as the
International Salt Company, the parent organization being the
International of New Jersey. Included in it were various salt
plants in New York State, in Michigan, and the Avery Salt

Mine in Louisiana. Also the Retsof mine in New York State which with Avery constituted the Nation's only salt mining operations.

International approached Joy Morton with a proposal that he head up their western group of operations, to be known as International of Illinois. Feeling that, as the operating director, he could still have the independence and freedom of movement necessary to conduct the business in his own way, Morton accepted. With his salt plants going both in Kansas and Michigan, he was the logical man to take over the post. Moreover, his long and successful work as agent for the entire Michigan Salt Association gave him what in present-day parlance would be called an additional "in."

During the years in which Morton did business as the International Salt Company of Illinois, he continued to operate just as before. He now had warehouses not only in Chicago, but in Milwaukee, Sheboygan, and Duluth-Superior. Expanding plant facilities and a growing force of workmen meant, of course, an increasing business—much of it in new territory.

For five years the International of Illinois continued. In that period the first really modern salt plants were built—plants that burned coal for fuel and were equipped with modern vacuum pans. The first of these was built at Cayuga, near Ithaca, New York. Another was put up at Watkins, New York, on the design of a German engineer named Faller. Faller believed he could make coarse salt by the vacuum pan method. It didn't work out as he expected. He did not get coarse salt; but his pans did well on the regular vacuum pan product.

Faller had another idea—a good one. Instead of putting salt as it came from the evaporator into pans to drain and dry, he tried to get rid of the excess moisture by suction. Although his efforts were not successful, the general idea has since been adopted almost universally by the industry.

In this same period International of Illinois built modern salt plants at Hutchinson, Kansas, and Ludington, Michigan, and the plant at Port Huron, Michigan, was also acquired. The vacuum pans at these plants were around 12 feet in diameter—a great deal larger than the trial vacuum pans that Joseph Duncan built for the Worcester Salt Co. at Silver Springs, New York, in the early Eighties; and though efforts have been made to operate vacuum pans as large as 30 feet in diameter, results have not been as satisfactory as with somewhat smaller pans. We shall read more of Duncan, later on.

So, all things considered, very definite progress in the techniques of making, storing and distributing salt came out of the last years of the nineteenth and the early years of the twentieth centuries—progress from which the entire nation would profit.

CHAPTER NINETEEN

A LITTLE GIRL
AND A BIG UMBRELLA

A NATIONAL POLL of housewives conducted two or three years ago revealed some interesting sidelights on America's buying habits. Questioned as to certain standard food brands, more than 90% of the 4,000 housewives interrogated gave answers that indicated their familiarity with Morton's free-running table salt, although many of that number replied merely:

"The can with the little umbrella girl on it!"

Thus does a familiar trade-mark impress itself upon the national consciousness. America has seen this tiny girl smiling out from pages of magazines and newspapers; down from billboards, posters, car-cards, from blotters and handbills, no less than from labels on the merchandise itself. The story of this trade-mark—little Miss Morton trudging cheerily along in the pouring rain with a can of free-running salt under her arm, and the motto "When it Rains it Pours"—goes back a number of years—to 1910.

There are many stories as to how she originated so this is a good place to put down the real facts about her birth. But first let us tell you some more about her family.

The century was still very young, you will recall, when Joy Morton put his plants and business into the International Salt Co. of Illinois, western group of the International of New Jersey, and took over the management. The western division was profitable from the start. The eastern division—International Salt Co. of New York—had embarked on the ambitious expansion program noted above. The heavy expenditures had lead to financial difficulties, the outcome of which was that Joy Morton offered to buy from the New Jersey company all Michigan and Kansas properties and businesses.

Thus was born the Morton Salt Company, new in name but old in organization and tradition. The company acquired the two new vacuum-pan plants in Ludington, Michigan, and Hutchinson, Kansas, as well as the Port Huron, Michigan, plant. All of these plants had both vacuum pan and grainer equipment, the latter being used to produce the medium or flake grain salt. Port Huron and Hutchinson had refining, drying and packing equipment; Ludington produced principally bulk salt for shipment to the warehouses on the western shore of Lake Michigan. The capacities of the plants were about equal.

Also included was the old plant at Wyandotte, earliest of Morton's manufacturing operations. It was soon shut down.

A number of the older plants in Kansas were also abandoned as most of them had old-fashioned open pans from which salt had to be "lifted" or raked by hand.

In addition to the three warehouses in Chicago there were two at Milwaukee, Wisconsin, one at Sheboygan, Wisconsin; and one at Toledo, Ohio.

Besides these manufacturing facilities Morton took on the sales agency for the Retsof Mining Company, then the only rock salt producer in the East, and another operation at Avery Island, Louisiana.

More important, however, than the actual physical assets thus brought into the firm, was a high degree of something intangible though no less real on that account. I refer to the quality of goodwill, the reputation for integrity and high standing which had been built up through the sixty years since 1848, when the ancestor of the firm—Alonzo Richmond, fresh from Onondaga— had begun to serve the salt buyers of the West. For, although the firm name had been changed several times, the general policies continued as they always had been and the salt trade in general recognized that fact.

The stockholders of the new company were Joy Morton, president and largest owner; his brother Mark Morton, vice president; his son Sterling Morton, secretary; and Daniel Peterkin, treasurer. Three others—C. S. Ostrom, A. G. Warren and Preston McGrain, all employes of long standing—completed the list of directors.

Training Ground for Executives

"I can raise better men than I can hire.!"

So said the great meat packer, Gustavus F. Swift. And so Joy Morton might well have said, late in his life, glancing over the list of men whom he, from time to time, had trained in the organization.

Parenthetically, it's rather an astounding thing, that so many, once they have joined the Morton force, have remained, assuming through the years successively higher responsibilities as they prove their ability to undertake them.

Not that the salt business is a bed of roses. Any man who has come into the Morton organization, with that belief, has soon had the wool snatched rudely from his eyes. Veterans in the salt business know that it is easier to make salt than to sell it. The production end also has its full share of problems, obstacles, setbacks, and discouragements.

In acquiring plants and agencies, Mr. Morton usually took over the operating and administration personnel as well. In many cases these men became important factors in the Morton organization. Chief among these was the man who was to succeed Joy Morton as president—Daniel Peterkin. Under his administration the company continued its growth and maintained its leadership in the industry. Under him also important improvements were made in manufacturing processes to turn out more and better salt.

Mr. Peterkin joined the firm while it was yet Joy Morton & Company, in 1896, coming from the Chicago sales office of Standard Salt Co. of Ohio, which Morton took over in that year. Not many years earlier Peterkin, then a young man from the "hielands" of Scotland, had come to America—like many another, to seek his fortune. Unlike many another, he actually found it. His childhood home had been in the old granite city of Aberdeen where his father, who was drowned while Dan was a youngster, had a real estate business.

The Chicago World's Fair of 1893 was going full tilt when young Peterkin landed in New York and began working on such odd jobs as he could find. But '93 was a panic year and jobs were scarcer in New York than elsewhere. So when the chance presented itself for him to go west—west in those days being Indianapolis, Indiana—he seized it. His first job there was with Kingan & Co., meat packers. From there he went to Chicago and was employed as a clerk by the Standard Salt Co. at the time Morton acquired the Chicago end of the business. Peterkin, with two others who afterwards rose to high positions with Morton, was among those who came over to the old office on Illinois Central Pier No. 1.

After a while, Mr. Morton found he needed a private secretary. Dan asked for the place. The boss looked at and through him with that unswerving gaze which seemed to look right through a man's innermost mind.

"Can you write shorthand?" the boss demanded.

Peterkin did not reply as did the musical aspirant who, asked if he could play the violin, said he didn't know, he'd never tried it. Instead, the young Scot answered:

"No sir. I don't know shorthand but I can learn it in two weeks." And to prove it, he started at once to night school. Two weeks later he actually took over the job as secretary to the boss. From then on, his rise with the company was steady and sure.

A man of keen business insight and an uncanny ability to get immediately at the heart of any business problem, Mr. Peterkin possessed a great reticence and quietness of manner. At first, it is said, you were likely to think him cold. Once his interest was aroused, however, he would enter with enthusiasm into anything that engaged his attention. Employees who worked under Mr. Peterkin during the years when he was treasurer of the Morton Salt Company, and later its President, still speak of his unswerving fairness in all matters. He was known to appreciate and reward loyalty in his men. The door of his office always stood open; he would listen to any employee's story.

In correspondence, say salt men, Mr. Peterkin could express in half a page what the average business man required two pages to put over. This quality, and his ability to go straight to the heart of any problem no matter how knotty, was buttressed by the fact that he set about at once to learn the salt business at first hand, both executive and operations ends. He assumed the presidency of the company in 1931 when Mr. Morton became chairman of the board. . . .

But we are jumping ahead too fast. Returning to the beginning of the Morton Salt Company in 1910, the company made its bow with a gesture which won wide-spread public approval; it made a sweeping reduction in prices. And since the nationwide salt trade was in a very disturbed condition just then, the effect of the move was quieting and salutary. This kind of introduction brought the name and policies of the new company very forcibly before the salt-buying public.

A new age in the retail food business was then just dawning. Growing national awareness of the need for greater sanitation was ushering in the era of packaged foods. Those old-fashioned dirt collectors—the open cracker box, the salt, sugar, and flour barrels—along with other bulk food containers, began to move into the discard. On grocery shelves appeared rows and rows of neatly wrapped and packaged retail foods. This form of merchandising possessed a great popular appeal. Food dealers everywhere began to capitalize on it. Quick to realize the trend, Morton set about to develop a quality package for its salt, and a quality product also.

Up to that time, there had been no real attempt to obtain uniformity in salt quality or texture. Table salt? Oh, yes, there was table salt of a kind—the ordinary product of the evaporating pans, dried and placed in convenient-size packages, boxes, or cloth bags. The purity of the product varied widely, depending upon the place of manufacture and the process used.

Morton technical men set to work to produce a table salt having the most desirable quality of not clogging. Several years of experimentation followed. Then the chemists came up with the answer: less than two per cent of other chemicals added to the carefully screened and graded cube-shaped crystal produced by the vacuum pans under carefully controlled conditions did the trick. It kept the salt from caking except under the most extreme circumstances. Moreover, the added ingredients were in themselves healthful and beneficial to the human body.

The details of producing this free-running salt are described in another chapter of this volume.

Next was needed a package to contain the new salt. A moisture-proof fiber can finally was chosen and, in collaboration with one of the big can companies, a handy "pouring spout" was devised for the top of the can. Then, the article was ready for market.

The question of a name for the new product now became important. Morton, fully convinced that now at last he had the finest article in the salt line, said it would be called simply Morton's Salt. He went on to say that the best guarantee of the integrity of a product is the fact that the maker puts his own name on it. In other words, that he is convinced the product is so good he is willing to stake his personal reputation on it.

Many ingenious suggestions were made but were all vetoed in favor of the simple firm name. Up to that time no thought had been given to a trade-mark or advertising slogan. However, an advertisng agency was called in consultation as to how the new salt could best be introduced. They suggested twelve advertisements, one each month for a year, in a magazine going to the housewives of the country.

In accordance with this suggestion they brought in a series of twelve drawings they suggested be used. They also had additional drawings in reserves as alternates.

A conference was held in the office of Sterling Morton, who had charge of developing the new product. One of the alternate sketches was of a little girl walking in the rain under an umbrella. As Morton had a young daughter at the time, it attracted his attention.

It told the whole story—there was the falling rain indicating damp weather. The salt running out of the package under the child's arm told the message the company wanted to put across—the salt would pour even in damp weather.

The little girl was an appealing figure to anyone, particularly to the housewife. Morton immediately said this would make an excellent trade-mark and gave instructions that the printing of labels be stopped until the new design could be worked out. The salt which had already been put on the market had merely the plain heading "Morton's Salt." It was, however, blue and white, that color having been chosen by Joy Morton; he had used those colors in Argo Starch, a product he had put on the market from the Nebraska City Starch Works, which he controlled. When later taken over by the Corn Products Co., that great organization retained "Argo" as its leading starch brand. Mr. Morton had found the blue package an excellent one in appearance, durability and freedom from soil when handling.

(Incidentally he adopted the name "Argo" for his starch so that it would come first on the alphabetical price lists gotten out by the wholesale grocers all over the country.)

So now the name, the package, the color of the label and the trade-mark had been settled. There remained only the advertising slogan to develop. Under the picture of the little girl as submitted were the words: "Even in Rainy Weather it Flows Freely." The conferees decided that was too long for a slogan.

"What we need is something short like Ivory Soap—It Floats," remarked Sterling Morton. Going to work on that there soon developed the slogan "Morton's Salt—It Pours." Then someone quoted the old proverb—"It never rains but it pours." Morton vetoed that because of the negative. After a round-the-table discussion, the old adage was twisted into "When it Rains it pours" —words that have since become nationally known.

Advertising men have many stories of how this slogan and trade-mark evolved. It has even been said that a large sum of money was paid to someone who came in with the suggestion. This is the sort of myth which naturally grows up around an outstanding article.

The actual development of the slogan and trade-mark, however, are as here described. The Morton men around the table took a rejected picture and legend of the advertising agency and developed it into one of the country's best known trade-marks and slogans.

CHAPTER TWENTY

A TALL TREE FALLS

THE ENTIRE SALT producing world was saddened in the spring of 1934 by the death of Joy Morton at the age of seventy-eight. For so long a time had he been the dominant figure in the industry that his passing seemed something out of the ordinary course of nature. It was as though a landmark, long familiar on the business horizon, had been removed. Few if any of his associates and competitors could recall a time when he had not been the power to reckon with. In Chicago—where long ago he had come to begin his career as a salt broker and manufacturer and where, during his long and active life, he had become one of the outstanding citizens—hundreds of friends and associates lamented him.

Four years earlier Mr. Morton had retired as president, becoming the company's first chairman of the board. Into his place stepped the man who as a youth forty years earlier had been the boss' stenographer and private secretary, and who had ever since been growing in stature even as the company had been developing and expanding—Daniel Peterkin.

Through this well at Port Huron, Michigan, salt from 2000 feet
below ground is pumped up as brine. By evaporation, the brine is
turned into salt again.

Huge settling tanks, 30 feet deep, in which the brine from below ground is purified.

Here is a battery of vacuum pans, cone shaped at top and bottom, in which granulated salt is made.

Tons of salt pass through this filter dryer every hour.

Next, the salt goes through this rotary kiln and the last trace of moisture is removed.

Cans of table salt, filled and sealed by machines, move in a long procession down the production line.

Machines fill 100-pound sacks for agricultural and industrial purposes.

The Chairman, however, still retained an intimate association with the active conduct of the business, suggesting and deciding important matters of policy.

Relieved of the heavier burden, Mr. Morton now had time to do a good many things he had long wanted to do. He had more opportunity for reading and travel, and for being with his family. Best of all, he could now bring to reality a dream which had been his since boyhood days in almost treeless Nebraska.

From his father, J. Sterling Morton, Joy inherited an intense love of trees. In the father, that love had found expression in the establishment of Arbor Day as a national holiday. In the son, it grew into a living green monument—an extensive woodland preserve 25 miles west of Chicago, through which run lovely drives. On this 800-acre tract Mr. Morton as early as 1921 began to assemble tree specimens from all parts of the globe—the nucleus of an arboretum. This he intended for the public; an area to be devoted to practical scientific research, arboreculture and horticulture. Nature lovers everywhere, hearing of it, have since come from far and near to study the 4800 species, varieties and hybrids of woody plants of all parts of the world, as well as to consult the well-stocked library.

It was Mr. Morton's long-range intention, and since ably furthered by his estate, to grow on this arboretum every known tree, shrub and vine that would flourish in the climate of northern Illinois. This is still the objective of the self-perpetuating institution which he endowed liberally.

Here, in his well-earned leisure, the aging salt king spent much of the last period of his life, walking about under the trees, watching the horticulturists and landscape men at work, pointing out to friends and visitors with the enthusiasm which only a nature-lover can know the peculiarities or beautiful markings of this leaf, or that bush or bloom.

And that other monument to him—the salt company which he founded and, so to speak, raised by hand—it, too, continued to develop through the years following his retirement in 1930 and his death in 1934. The present company bears about as much resemblance to the small salt agency which Alonzo Richmond set up on Lake Street a hundred years ago as the great city in which it is located bears to the ugly, unpaved, outpost village on which Richmond first cast his eye in 1848.

One hundred years ago! Chicago then had less than 25,000 people. Some two-, three- and four-story business houses stood along the board sidewalks. There was a miserable drainage system, a superfluity of mud; but unlimited energy. For all the vigor and drive of its inhabitants, however, few could have dreamed that a city of 4,000,000 would, within a century, emerge from that pioneer community. Yet there it stands today—premier city of the midwest, the better-than-hoped-for realization of its founders.

Nor, by the same token, could Alonzo Richmond or his immediate successors who ran the agency that in time became Morton Salt Company, have entertained the least idea that their organization would grow to become one of the world's largest salt producers: a company employing 3500 people and having a system of 12 widely separated producing plants, branches in all major cities and warehouses strategically located for expeditious delivery.

Joy Morton very early visualized a national system of distribution. His effort, therefore, from the time he bought his first plant in Kansas and began manufacturing, had been directed towards that objective. As he went along, experience taught him many things. For example, getting your product from a distant refining plant and moving it to a large central warehouse; then taking it out again for delivery to the trade as needed, involved long hauls which inevitably shot up the price the consumer had to pay.

Salt is a heavy bulky commodity and the freight rates on it are high compared to the value of the product itself. For that reason, each salt producing field has a certain territory in which it alone can economically supply the salt needs. Enlightened self interest, therefore, no less than the desire to furnish better service, demanded that the Company set up plants and warehouses each located with a view to servicing contiguous localities.

Further impetus was lent to this demand, following 1910, by the company's national advertising campaign: orders began coming in from all parts of the country. That made it imperative, if effective and competitive nationwide service were to be supplied, that the manufacturing and distribution facilities keep pace with the advertising by further development of production of facilities.

This policy is today generally followed by all large American businesses which provide nation-wide service. It was Joy Morton, pioneer salt man, and Daniel Peterkin, and others like them who pointed the way and set the pace in that direction which has had so wholesome an effect upon modern merchandising.

During the years that have passed since 1910, the company has followed the policy of acquiring additional operations when the time and opportunity warranted it. By 1910, you recall, it had plants going both in Michigan and Kansas. Eight years later Morton began getting salt from Burmester, Utah. That was the genesis of its Great Salt Lake activity which today comprises an important section of its western business.

Successively other plants have been added by purchase, or construction. Among these may be mentioned:

An evaporating plant at Grand Saline, Texas, in 1920. A new large salt mine, near Grand Saline, in 1928. A new and extensive evaporating and solar treating plant on the Pacific Coast, near Newark, California, in 1925. A mine at Kanapolis, Kansas in 1941. An eastern plant, the Worcester Salt Company at Silver Springs, New York, in 1943. An evaporating plant at Cleveland, Ohio in 1944. A mine in one of Louisiana's salt domes, a few miles from Avery Island where, at Petite Anse in 1862, one of Judge Avery's negroes first discovered the presence of rock salt in the United States; and an evaporating plant at Akron, Ohio in 1948.

Coming down to date, the picture of the company today is one of nation-wide extent—a smoothly functioning, well articulated organization of many parts, drawing its supply from eight states: Michigan, Kansas, New York, Ohio, Texas, California, Louisiana and Utah; maintaining branch sales offices in 25 major American cities, most of which have warehouses handily located to supply the local trade.

The Minerals Year Book for 1946 lists 74 salt-producing plants in the United States. Many of these are but small and isolated operations serving their immediate localities. Some are chemical manufacturing companies which on occasion sell the by-product salt that results from their processes. Included in these are the Pennsylvania Salt Company plant at Wyandotte, Michigan; and the Columbia Chemical Company of Barberton, Ohio, a subsidiary of the Pittsburgh Plate Glass Company.

Then there are the other large producers, with well established plants and organizations — companies which share with Morton and Morton's affiliate plants the task of keeping the bulk of America's salt needs supplied. A brief summary by states would read this way:

New York: The International Salt Company has plants at Watkins Glen (the location also of the Watkins Salt Company), Ludlowville and Retsof. At Ludlowville, also, is the Cayuga Rock Salt Company.

Ohio: The Colonial Salt Company, a subsidiary of General Foods Company, at Akron. At Pomeroy are the Excelsior Salt Company, and the Pomeroy Salt Company (plant nearby at Minersville).

Michigan: Manistee Salt Works at Manistee; at the town of St. Louis, the Michigan Chemical Company; at St. Clair, the Diamond Crystal Salt Company, also a General Foods affiliate. International has a rock salt mine under the city of Detroit.

West Virginia: In the Kanawha Valley, J. Q. Dickinson & Company at Malden, near Charleston. On the Ohio River, the

Ohio River Salt Company at Mason. At New Martinsville, the Natrium plant of the Pittsburgh Plate Glass Company.

Louisiana: The Jefferson Island Salt Company is at Jefferson Island; the Gordy Salt Company at Franklin; the Carey Salt Company has one of its plants at Winnfield. International has an operation at Avery Island.

Kansas: At Lyons is the plant of the American Salt Company. Carey Salt Company has plants and mines at both Hutchinson and Lyons. At Kanapolis is the Independent Salt Company. The Barton Salt Company operates at Hutchinson.

California: The Imperial Salt Company plant is located at Nyland. The Leslie Salt Company has plants at Alvorado, Newark, and Redwood City, as well as a production plant known as the California Rock Salt Company at Amboy, in the Mohave desert; the Monterey Bay Salt Company makes solar salt at Moss Landing, near Monterey. The Chula Vista plant of the Western Salt Company, near San Diego, makes large quantities of coarse salt.

Texas: The United Salt Company of Houston has a plant at Hockley.

Oklahoma: Oklahoma Salt Industries, Inc., have operations at Sayre.

CHAPTER TWENTY-ONE

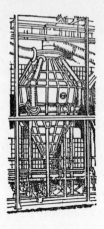

SALT MAKING—
MODERN METHODS

SALT IS NO LONGER *just salt*. We have come a long, long distance since our grandparents' day when the only refining that salt knew was "breaking big ones into little ones." In those days it was served up to you on the table damp, with all its impurities intact. The same salt that cured meat in the smokehouse and was fed to farm animals also graced the family board.

As we read along we shall see that there are now many kinds, grades, and types of salt—each developed to meet certain demands of a complex, modern civilization. To illustrate: the salt that is used to ice railroad refrigerator cars is definitely not that which goes into the baking of our bread, the pickling of cucumbers, and the preparation of other foods. Salt that is employed in "pickling" ingots at the steel mills bears little resemblance to the table salt that flows easily and in a fine stream from your salt cellar.

166

With the spread of civilization and settlement, America's uses of salt have multiplied until there is hardly any facet of industry, agriculture, or home life into which good old dependable sodium chloride does not enter. In another part of this book is a partial list of these uses. Even a partial list is long; it would be impracticable to make a complete one.

Now making salt to meet all these multifarious needs requires different systems of manufacture no less than specially designed and intricate machinery—the result of years of effort. The grain structure of the salt is determined by the process by which it is refined and prepared for distribution.

To understand just how modern salt is made, suppose we visit several of these plants from which Morton obtains its salt and take a look at the steps in making the different grades obtained from three unchanging sources—wells, mines, the sea.

Morton gets more salt from wells than from anywhere else. You will recall how the early operators at Syracuse, Kanawha, and other centers, sank wells and drew up natural brine which became increasingly stronger the deeper they dug down for it. Salt makers still sink wells. But now they drill straight down to the deep-lying beds of rock salt. It was from these salt beds, in most cases, that the natural brine came up to the surface in springs. Rather than depend upon natural brines, modern salt men make brine for themselves—make it out of rock salt and then turn it back into refined salt. How? We shall see.

Let's go back to the year 1883 and to an almost forgotten genius by the name of George Smith of Saltvale, N. Y. Saltvale lies in the rock salt belt of Wyoming County in which borings for rock salt were first made in 1877. Only 10 miles to the South lies Silver Springs, location of the modern plant of the Worcester Salt Company. Smith was a practical salt man with advanced ideas. Having drilled down more than 1,500 feet, through layers of soil, clay, shale, limestone, and slate, he came to rock salt. But how to get it out? His well was only about 10 inches in diameter. Sinking a mine shaft in those days to 1,500 feet and sending down miners to dig out the salt with pick and shovel would not of course have been practical. For one thing, it would have been too fearfully expensive.

It was while Smith mulled this question over in his mind that the idea of sending a stream of fresh water down and letting it dissolve the rock salt occurred to him. From that germ of an idea, he evolved a workable plan. Into his 10-inch well he sank a pipe down to the top of the salt bed. Next he sank a smaller pipe inside the larger one, down almost to the bottom of the salt bed. Then he shot a stream of water straight down between the smaller and the larger pipes.

Far below the fresh water spread out into the salt bed around the base of the pipe dissolving the rock salt. Leaving the dissolving to continue for a time, Smith then attached pumps and brought the brine surging up through the center pipe—brine stronger than any yet put to use commercially.

"The advantage of my hydraulic method of salt mining is not only that it's cheaper," said George Smith, "but that it assures us of a constant flow of strong brine. Sea water has only a quarter pound of salt in each gallon; and the Dead Sea in Palestine from two to two-and-one-third pounds. But my process brings up dissolved rock salt that contains two-and-two-thirds pounds in every gallon."

George Smith's method, with some improvements, is that used in many refining plants today.

We'll now see how salt makers turn that brine back into salt. At Port Huron, Michigan, the big refining plant lies in the midst of fourteen wells which supply a continuous stream of brine under the urging of a pumping system powerful enough to furnish water to a city of a half-million people.

Straight from the wells the brine comes to the plant by pipes, flowing into deep settling tanks—vats of 215,000 gallons each. There chemists test it as to its strength and the quantity of foreign matter it contains. That foreign matter has got to come out! For that, among other things, is what modern salt refining does—removes impurities. Step number one is to let the brine remain in those first tanks until the insoluble matter carried along in the brine settles out—sinks to the bottom—leaving a tolerably clear liquid. Then a careful chemical treatment further purifies it until, should you throw a coin in the vat, you could see it clearly on the bottom, thirty feet below—so transparent is the brine.

Sparkling clear, it is now ready for its next step toward salt. Now there are two methods by which that brine may be made into salt. Both are evaporation processes and both are constantly used to obtain different types of products. For a table salt—the high grade free-running cube article such as the little Umbrella Girl represents—the brine will go into vacuum pans. If a flake salt is desired—a salt known to the trade as "medium" and used for many purposes—the brine will go into what are known as grainer pans.

Let the Vacuums Do the Work!

We'll follow through with the vacuum pans first.

The vacuum process for salt making is the invention of another old-time salt boiler. His name was Joseph M. Duncan, and like George H. Smith, inventor of the "hydraulic" process, he came from New York. Duncan was born in Syracuse while the Mexican War was still going on. His first job was boiling salt in his home town. Soon the new rock-salt industry of Wyoming County drew him, like many another Syracuse man, from the declining Onondaga brine fields to try his luck in the salt town of Warsaw. In 1885, Duncan bought out a small plant and began experimenting. He had an idea that if you could boil your brine in an air-tight cooker (a vacuum pan) under lowered pressure, you could make it more cheaply and get a better product.

Already utilized in making sugar, the vacuum pan idea was based upon a simple scientific principle, namely, that water boils more quickly in a high altitude (i. e., under lower atmospheric pressure) than at sea level. Therefore less fuel is required to make water boil on the top of Pike's Peak than on the seashore; but as the temperature of the vaporization (or boiling point) is much lower, don't try to boil eggs up there!

Accordingly Joe and his brother built an air-tight pan—the first vacuum pan ever built for salt making. It was a little one, only seven feet in diameter, and no great shakes as a success. Duncan found that gypsum in the brine so coated the tubes through which it passed that he had to shut down every few hours and clean them. However, later developments in salt-making technique have overcome this difficulty. Duncan's next pan had all the essentials used in the modern complicated vacuum-pan process.

Another improvement is that modern pans are used in "batteries" of three or more—a great saving in fuel, since by regulating pressures and temperatures the vapor produced by making the salt in the first pan can be made to boil the brine in the second pan, and so on. Live steam in the boilers thus goes only to the first pan, or "first effect," as salt makers call it.

Stand here in this big room and look above you. Those four giant-size inverted cast-iron cones which reach down from the ceiling are the bottoms of the vacuum pans. They are twenty feet in diameter at the biggest part, and so tall that their tops extend to the next floor above you. Up there you would see that their tops also are cone-shaped, the upper cones pointing upward. Between the bases of the two cones is a thick doughnut-shaped section called the steam belt. This steam belt extends far into the tank, leaving an opening or well (like the doughnut's hole) some four feet in diameter in the center.

Between the well and the tank's outer rim, this steam belt is pierced by hundreds of small upright copper tubes. It works this way: Steam, in the first pan, becomes hot vapor in the succeeding pans and circulates constantly around the tubes, making them intensely hot. The brine circulates *up* through the hot tubes and, as it passes through, is heated above its boiling point at the pressure in that pan. Look through a window on a platform from which the operation is controlled; you can see in there brine boiling and dancing around the upper part of the cone. It circulates constantly, down through the well, up through the tubes, its downward movement being accelerated by a propeller just under the well. A remarkable change has taken place within that evaporator. You saw the brine coming in and going *up* through the steam belt. But when it comes down, it contains innumerable cube-shaped crystals.

As the salt crystals are formed inside the pan, they sink on down to the bottom of the lower cone and are carried by enclosed pumps to the next step of refining, which is drying. A machine known as a filter dryer takes hold of the wet salt; so called because inside this dryer powerful fans blow filtered hot air through it. That reduces its wetness to about 2 percent.

In former times a salt containing only 2 percent moisture would have been considered an exceptionally fine commercial article. Wet salt, as recorded, used to be constantly marketed and people accepted it as a matter of course. Not so today! The last smidgen of wetness must come out of high-grade salt. You'll see how it's done. The rotary dryer is the next machine to get in its licks—that long cylinder, eight feet in diameter, whirling around over there. As the salt passes through it, an intense heat plays over it while the cylinder turns, the salt kept in motion by being picked up by revolving blades and dropped again through the heat with each revolution. From this end, look into the rotary dryer. See! It is extremely hot in there. And although there is no flame, you begin to realize what the old phrase "refining by fire" means. When the salt emerges, it is bone dry, and ready for the next step.

A conveyor belt next hustles the dry salt along to be graded to the exact size of crystal desired. Other grades of salt, you understand, besides the table grade are made by the vacuum process. How are they separated? By shaking screens—nine of them—through which the salt passes and, as the different size meshes winnow out the crystals of each separate size, they fall down into the proper bin to await packing.

We follow the table salt—which is carefully screened to assure uniform-size crystals—and see it going into its proper bin. Now for packaging!

This business of putting salt in the familiar round can is a most engrossing sight to the layman. Thus far, from the well through the successive steps of production, human hand has not touched the product, either as brine or salt. The same applies to packaging. Throughout, salt making is a scientific, machine operation.

A large supply of the empty cans is kept on hand at each plant. Their spouts mechanically opened and ready for filling, these cans are automatically fed into a machine which marches them along in a steady procession, following a straight course, swinging around curves, turning corners, and finally passing under the bin spouts. Because of its free-running quality, the salt slips down into the cans as they pass beneath the filling machine; the machine putting into each can the exact amount of salt, down to the fractional part of an ounce. Another machine seals and still another labels the can. The filled cans then go to be packed by machine into cartons for shipment.

Somewhere along the salt-production line—although we haven't seen it—something has been done to improve the quality of the product—in certain special ways. Two things, in fact. First, about 2% magnesium carbonate—a chemical, by the way, which is itself definitely healthful—has been mixed with the salt. Reason: this further insures it against clogging or packing down in damp weather by forming a protective coating over each and every separate grain, thus keeping it from sticking to its neighbor. A specially constructed machine insures that exactly the right amount goes into each pound of salt.

When buying salt in the round can, you have doubtless noticed some of the cans marked "Iodized." There's a reason, and the reason involves some explanation. In putting together the various ingredients that make up the crust of the earth's surface, Nature has showed a lavish hand in most respects. In some instances, however, she has shown some discrimination in that the elements necessary to human health are not all included in the soil of certain regions. Experience shows that the disease known as goiter—the enlarging of the thyroid glands in the throat—occurs more frequently in those areas where Nature has not included a sufficient quantity of iodine so that the vegetables, etc., from these districts are likewise short of iodine. Health authorities discovered that where this iodine deficiency could be replaced, the incidence of goiter could be minimized or even prevented.

Public health officials and state health authorities therefore talked the matter over with Morton some years ago, with the result that potassium iodide was added to the salt destined for areas where more iodine was needed, and at no extra charge. One gets an enlightening idea of how small an amount goes into an ordinary round can of salt when it is explained that one-fifth pound of iodide ingredient is sufficient *for one ton of salt*. Therefore, the addition of this chemical, like the magnesium carbonate, is not trusted to human hands. Each can of iodized salt contains its proper quota—no more, no less.

So much for how free-running table salt is made. Table salt accounts for only about 4% of America's 9,000,000 tons a year salt consumption (315,000,000 bushels). There are many uses to which salt is put—industrial, commercial, and agricultural—for which other kinds of salt are used. Flake salt, known to the trade as "medium," is a product of the grainer-pan process. These grainers—they are operated in most of the plants which have the vacuum pans—are the outgrowth of the small pans which George H. Patrick invented in 1835. Patrick, as recounted in the chapters on Kanawha, was a Syracuse man. His pans, however, were not well received by the makers of Onondaga salt, but they did come into general use all through the Kanawha Valley, putting the kettles into the discard.

Patrick's first boiling pans were cast iron, about nine feet long, four feet wide and eight inches deep. Bolted together in a series, the whole would be called a furnace. In these pans direct fire heat boiled the brine and evaporated the water. There was a wooden steam chest over the boiling pans which caught the steam and sent it through big wooden pipes into smaller copper pipes which passed through other pans known as settlers and grainers. In these latter pans the salt formed . . . .

Now come over into another large building and we will look at the rows of grainer pans. Instead of little nine-foot fellows, these modern grainer pans are giants, each about one hundred feet long, two feet deep and twelve feet wide. Remember the brine as we saw it in its purified state, in those big tanks thirty feet deep? Well, just as brine was drawn from those tanks into the vacuum pans, so it is also drawn into the grainers for making of medium or flake salt.

Suspended in the brine are coils of four-inch pipe through which steam constantly circulates, keeping it at boiling temperature. That is a very important matter in making salt by the grainer pan process—keeping your brine at the same temperature! As little as a two-percent variation—and bing!—you won't get the grain of salt that you wish. The size of the grain, you see, is determined by the degree of heat used. A high temperature makes a fine grain; low temperature a coarse grain.

Now standing here by the side of these big pans you will notice splotches that appear briefly on the surface like little islands on a pond, and then vanish. That's salt in the making. The crystals, as they rise to the surface and collect there in masses, become too heavy to keep afloat; they sink of their own weight out of sight. The salt collects on the bottom of the pan, but it doesn't stay there. If your eyes are good, you can see blades or paddles the width of the pan, moving slowly and unceasingly through the brine. Those are feathering rakes that keep pushing the salt on the bottom toward the back end of the pan and up on to an inclined board or platform to drain. After a while it, too, will go into the plant for drying and packing.

Besides the round can, the boxes, sacks, and bags in which are packed the products of the grainer and vacuum pans, there is still another important product which requires no packing. This is the salt block or the "stock block."

Farmers and stock raisers, aware that animals must have salt and have it in abundance, place salt in the fields where the cattle graze and in the stalls to be taken as needed. Like the human body, animal constitutions demand a constant supply of salt to replace that drained out in sweat and other excretion. Only the animal itself knows just the proper amount required. He will not take more than is necessary, you can depend upon it! Place salt where it is easily accessible and the animal will partake of it to the satisfaction of itself and the profit of its owner.

It used to be the practice for farmers and stockmen to put a big chunk of rock salt in the field or pasture, or wherever it would be handy for the animals. Of late years, however, salt makers have developed the specially prepared salt block for "free choice" feeding. In the same plants where you saw the various grades in the process of making, the salt blocks are produced by a huge press. A salt block weighs fifty pounds and in it a large quantity of salt crystals are solidified under a pressure of 1,000 pounds per square inch. The result looks rather like a smooth block of white marble.

These presses are largely automatic in operation and turn out a steady stream of blocks; no adhesive or binder is used, the compressed salt particles adhering to each other closely.

Smaller machines press salt into small blocks for the manger or other uses while still smaller ones make the familiar tablets useful in preventing heat fatigue in humans and for use in the canning factory.

CHAPTER TWENTY-TWO

SOLAR HARVEST

MAN, UNTOLD AGES AGO, turned for salt to the sea and other bodies of salt water. The American salt industry still obtains a part of its supply from the same source. Let's see how it is done.

From wide, level, solar ponds on the shores of Great Salt Lake in Utah and along San Francisco Bay in California, mighty salt crops are annually harvested. The word "harvest" is here aptly used. On so vast a scale is solar salt now produced that there is a kind of elemental grandeur in it—a rhythmic, annually recurring, seasonal procedure that reminds one in truth of the planting and reaping of wide grain fields.

Utah produces about 100,000 tons of salt annually, which is a far cry from the first primitive endeavors of the early Mormon settlers. You've already read how they got their salt. That summer of their arrival (1847) had not waned before most Mormon families had developed the practice of going down to the lake shore with kettles to "roll their own." Four or five men with

Through this big pipe and flume Great Salt Lake's briny water is pumped into the evaporating ponds at Saltair, Utah.

Gaunt machines harvest the salt from the ponds at the right season.
(Industrial Photos, Courtesy of Morton Salt Co.)

The wide spreading solar ponds of Utah.

Here you see a long pile of raw solar salt stacked and ready to go to the refining plant.

Loading solar salt to go into the refining plant.

A powerful machine presses salt into blocks for convenient stock feeding.

Not chunks of marble, but salt blocks which will be placed in fields to allow livestock to have free-choice feeding.

three kettles going could make forty bushels a day. What was the salt like?

With pardonable exaggerations, "it's just as white as Syracuse salt, and just as fine!" exclaims one proud Mormon pioneer, a statement that must be taken with a grain of the very stuff he describes.

Grinding salt between rollers, as previously described by Judge Elias Smith, or between upper and nether millstones—such was the extent of Utah's first salt refining. Many early housewives, according to Bill Langford, veteran salt maker at Saltair, near Salt Lake City (himself a descendant of a pioneer salt-making family), used to take home crude salt from the lake shore and grind the lumps in the old family coffee mill. That, Langford admits, was a long time before he was born.

In his fine book entitled, *The Great Salt Lake,** Dale Morgan says that from the first summer on, "There was rarely a time when fires were not burning under great iron kettles on the south shore of the lake." It remained for one Charlie White and his wife, however, to become "professionals." They built themselves a hut on the beach in 1849, lived there, and went into the business of furnishing salt for all who would buy.

When Captain Howard Stansbury made his Government survey of Great Salt Lake in 1849, he found that White's six kettles of sixty gallons each yielded 300 pounds of salt a day.

"I get a pail of salt from four pails of water in the summertime," Charlie White boasted to Stansbury, "and a pail from three pails of water in winter."

Morgan observes that White's statement could not have been very precise since a 25% salt solution is just about at saturation point, where precipitation begins.

"The unrefined lake salt was not perfect for all purposes," Morgan states rather superfluously. "The chemical analyst to whom Stansbury referred his samples discovered that in addition

---

*Bobbs-Merrill: 1947

to the 20% of common salt, the lake contained 2% of foreign salts, the most objectionable being chloride of lime and chloride of magnesia. These had a tendency to absorb moisture from the air, moistening and partially dissolving the common salt, so that when it was exposed to dry air or heat, it caked with a hard crust. A suggested remedy was to heap up the dry salt and sprinkle it with a concentrated brine from the lake at intervals of a few hours during a single day.

"Though the sodium chloride would not be dissolved, the chloride of calcium and magnesium would be drained off. By allowing the heaped-up salt to drain and dry at night, then spreading it to the sun for an hour or two next morning, the salt boilers could obtain a relatively pure salt."

"Alas for technology," Morgan continues, "the salt makers would not put themselves to any such trouble. The unrefined salt was good enough for them, and those who wanted a superior grade could import it from Liverpool. The result was that the lake salt often sold as low as 50 cents for a hundred pounds."*

It was for this reason that many Salt Lake City people began to order their salt from the East. But the railroad, extending its long and snaky line to the city in 1869, gave the lake salt industry a new lease on life. A firm called Smith, Housel, & Hopkins began that same year to produce on a large scale. We are not told how they improved their product, but improve it they certainly did. For in 1871 we find the *Salt Lake Herald* proudly boasting that the salt which now came from the lake was, for all the local prejudice about its being impure and unfit for commercial uses, "the peer of the world's finest—Turk's Island or Onondaga's."

"This thing should rise above the magnitude of an ordinary business," the *Herald* goes on didactically. "Salt Lake City, lying within a few miles of Great Salt Lake, should have enterprise

From THE GREAT SALT LAKE, by Dale Morgan, Copyright 1947, used by special permission of the publishers—Bobbs-Merrill Co.

enough to furnish all the salt required for culinary purposes in the same region; and should send carloads daily east and west by the railroad to meet the wants of millions of American citizens. . . . There is a vast trade here to be opened up. Where are the salt boilers?"

People may have been skeptical at the moment, but time has justified the *Herald's* prophecy. Salt Lake's refined product compares favorably with any salt made.

In 1873 one enterprising firm went into the matter to the serious extent of damming the mouth of a long lake bayou near the town of Kelton. Their idea was to place a windmill on shore, pump lake water into their pond and keep it full all summer. They thought that by this continuous and rapid evaporation they could make half a million bushels in a summer. The windmill idea in Utah has been lost sight of. And Dale Morgan wonders whether it was not a firm known as Barnes and Company, salt makers who later became important, that tried out the experiment. Wittingly or not, this Mormon firm was adopting a method tried out years before by early Dutch settlers on Long Island in New York. The windmill had been used to pump Atlantic Ocean water.

And speaking of Barnes and Company: it was in the '70's that some workmen at that plant had a visitation from Great Salt Lake's renowned sea serpent. They swore up and down they saw it just as others have sworn from time to time before and since. The salt workers claimed on affidavit that they had been "startled to hear an altogether frightful bellow on a July night in 1877. Looking out over the lake, they saw a huge and fearful creature having a body resembling that of a crocodile and a head resembling that of a horse. Even as they stared, it came charging at them.

"The men employed at the salt plant," Morgan goes on, "were men of superior minds. They knew exactly what to do in such circumstances. They stampeded up the mountain side and hid themselves securely amid the sage brush and scrub oak, remaining there throughout the night. By the time the sun rose the next morning, it seemed evident that the monster had gone about its business; and since such occurrences were all in the day's work, the men returned to their usual labor of extracting salt from lake brine."

The monster, it was reported, was forty feet long. . . .

Three important companies emerged in the 1880's from a number of scattering attempts of greater or less importance to make salt on the eastern shore of Great Salt Lake. These were the Jeremy Salt Company, the Inland Salt Company, and the Intermountain Salt Company. The last came into being in 1889. Jeremy failed after a few years. The other two merged under the name of Inland Crystal Salt Company.

When It's Harvest Time at Saltair!

Stand here on the shore of Great Salt Lake at Saltair beach in the summer sunshine. Behind you, twenty miles out a straight level highway, lies busy Salt Lake City. From your feet the lake dances and ripples away as far as you can see. The stark outline of Antelope Island cuts across your western vista, two miles off shore. Most likely some beathers, nearby at the Saltair pavilion, are enjoying a swim in these dense waters in which man floats without effort.

The far-stretching beaches shine like long strips of damask—sand and salt, sand and salt—dazzling white as far as the eye can reach. Those angular buildings over there in the distance comprise the plant where the crude salt, gathered from ponds at the lake shore, is refined to meet all the requirements of the various gradings, from fine table salt down to the bulk grades used for the most ordinary industrial purposes.

See that low, narrow, trestle-like structure, extending from the shore half a mile out into the lake to a small shed barely visible in the distance? That is a trough or flume, supported on "stilts." It carries the lake water from which salt will be made in the ponds. Five thousand gallons a minute, lake water pours through it, impelled by powerful pumps in the small shed out in the lake, the flow being governed by electric gadgets.

So thick with salt is the lake water in its natural state, it is necessary to mix it with fresh artesian water brought up through a pipe sunk in the lake bottom a half-mile off shore and thus "tone it down" so that it will not clog up the pumps. At the land end of its half-mile journey, the water rushes from the flume into a distributing channel and so on into the first of a series of ponds.

Now look over *this* way. Notice those wide, smooth sheets of water covering hundreds of acres. They have been divided off by lines of straight dikes which separate pond from pond as fences separate one field from another. There are two kinds of ponds necessary in the making of solar salt—concentration ponds and garden ponds. They are all less than twelve inches deep; a single pond covers many acres.

The inflowing stream of brine from the lake flows into the concentration ponds and spreads out over their wide extent. Here all suspended matter in the water—the insolubles—settles out. The remaining brine becomes increasingly heavy under Utah's bright sunlight. At last it concentrates to a point shown by the Baume-Scale salometer where the salt itself is about ready to crystallize out. Now it is sent on its next forward step—into the second series of ponds: the garden ponds.

There, as more and more of the water evaporates under the hot sun, the salt begins to crystallize out and drop to the bottom. This is a continuous process. As the water evaporates from the surface of the garden ponds, more concentrated brine is admitted to them and the salt depth in these ponds slowly increases.

Thus the salinity of the brine is kept at just about the salt precipitating point. Naturally the concentration of other soluble salts in the "mother liquor" gradually increases, and it is necessary from time to time to drain them off thus taking along all chemical salts but the sodium chloride which the salt makers are after.

As the sun continues its work, more and more salt crystallizes on the surface and then sinks, precipitating in a thick layer on the hard pond bottom. There it lies, waiting to be harvested.

The greatest care, of course, must be taken in governing the flow of brine from the concentration ponds to the garden ponds. That involves knowing just when the brine has reached the proper density to be moved on. Suppose rain comes? What of it! On this thick brine a "layer of rain" lies without mixing. It therefore does not dilute the brine. The salt men merely lower the dike gates enough to let out the rainwater into a drain ditch which carries it off. The process is rather like skimming the cream off a gigantic pan of milk.

There is a season for each step in making solar salt; a time, so to speak, to sow (that is, to turn water into the pond); a time to reap (that is, to gather in the salt) .

The harvest days are here! Salt harvesting demands special machines; and the men at the Saltair plant have developed a "harvester" such as Cyrus McCormick never dreamed of. It is designed specifically for salt work. A gaunt affair based on a Fordson tractor with a hydraulically-operated scoop on its nose which can be raised and lowered as needed.

You will see them—these harvesters—several at a time, scooting about over the ponds, swinging their scoops this way and that. Watch them! The scoop drops down to the salt floor. The tractor pushes it along until it is full. Then up comes the scoop with a ton of salt and the salt harvester speeds over to the pond's side, dumps its load into the hopper of another outlandish contraption known as a stacking conveyor, and hustles off for another load. The stacking conveyor moves slowly along, stacking the harvested salt in neat, continuous piles about eight feet high (windrows) near the railroad siding. On the siding, specially designed cars will be pushed out by a gasoline locomotive to pick up the salt as needed and roll it into the refining plant where a thorough system of drying, screening, and packing, as described previously, awaits it.

Day after day, twenty-four hours a day, the epic process goes
on—continuous, rhythmic, systematic. Utah's lake and Utah's hot
sun, plus modern technical methods, have made the prediction
of the *Salt Lake Herald* three-quarters of a century ago a reality.

Great Salt Lake supplies salt not only to Utah, but to many
adjacent states as well.

Brine of the Pacific

There is not a great deal of difference between the way solar
salt is gathered from Great Salt Lake and the way it is now taken
from San Francisco Bay, an arm of the Pacific Ocean in California. Pacific Ocean water naturally is not as saline as Great
Salt Lake water. That simply means that more gallons must be
evaporated to yield the equivalent amount of salt. The end product is the same.

In the production of vacuum-pan salt, however, at Morton's
westernmost plant located at Newark, California, the basic coarse
sea salt from San Francisco Bay undergoes a vigorous refining
This is accomplished by dissolving it in clear, fresh water.
A concentrated brine results. This, in turn, is chemically treated
and re-evaporated in vacuum pans in a manner similar to that
described in the chapter dealing with the Port Huron, Michigan,
plant. Free-running salt as well as the many other salt grades are
thus made for distribution in the entire West Coast area.

CHAPTER TWENTY-THREE

FROM SUBTERRANEAN
CRYSTAL HALLS

EVAPORATED SALT from the well. Solar salt from the sea. We have seen how both these are obtained. There is still another source which yields its quota to America's huge annual salt total—the mine, from which rock salt (halite) is dug.

Rock salt lies in beds or strata below the ground. At most places it is far down; at others, it occurs rather close to the surface. Various European countries have mined rock salt since the year 1000 A. D. The old Weiliczka mine near Crakow in Poland, as a single example, is still producing. Here in America salt men knew for years that there were beds of salt under the brine-producing areas of New York, Ohio, and other sections. But the stuff lay too far down for the earlier salt makers to get it out.

Deep drilling, made possible by Billy Morris' "slips-and-jars," came into use by 1840 and in time proved that the old boys were right in their belief. With the new drill you could bore all the way down to the salt bed hundreds, maybe thousands, of feet below the ground. Next, along came George Smith of upstate New York with his "hydraulic" system which dissolved the rock salt and brought it up as brine to be evaporated and refined. That happened first early in the 1880's.

But meanwhile, as you recall from earlier pages of this book, rock salt had been discovered down in Louisiana close enough to the surface to sink a mine shaft and send men and equipment down to bring out rock salt as such. Following the opening of this initial American salt mine—at Petite Anse on Avery Island in 1862 — other mines were sunk into other salt "domes" both in Texas and Louisiana; and down into the salt strata beneath the plains of Kansas. Other salt mines opened new production fields in New York State and Michigan, where beds lie at workable depths.

One large source of rock salt is the enormous mine at Grand Saline, Texas. We'd better go down and see how rock salt is taken out of that mine.

This Grand Saline mine is one of the newest and best equipped in the country. Its product is transparent, pure, and contains very little foreign matter. And that is an unusual quality in rock salt in its original state.

If you visit the town of Grand Saline, Texas, today, you will see on entering the city from either east or west, a huge black iron kettle mounted on a permanent foundation.

It is a monument which speaks of a time long past. It memorializes the industry which brought this enterprising community to wealth and prominence. For it was big kettles such as this that were used long ago, when natural brine oozing up in small quantities from the then unknown salt dome beneath the town, was boiled to make salt. Local historians explain that the Cherokee Indians got their salt here as long ago as 1834 when white men in these parts were as scarce as hen's teeth and the whole area was covered by a soggy salt marsh.

During Texas' heyday as an independent republic came the first commercially-minded salt makers, Jordan and McGee, bringing with them the big kettles. They were the initial settlers and gave their town its original name—Jordan's Salines.

In the next thirty years the infant industry became a going thing, employing many workmen. They followed the lead of Syracuse and Kanawha, piping their brine in hollow logs and setting their kettles in blocks. Although this early salt making never attained the dignity of a real industry, it did reach 100 barrels a day in the years just preceding the Civil War.

When the railroads reached Jordan Salines in 1872, the name was changed to Grand Saline and salt making took a forward leap. More wells were sunk during the next two decades and larger plants arose—grainer pans with steam coils through them to keep the brine boiling. These replaced the old kettles.

At Grand Saline, Now

A business and residential center, Grand Saline bears little resemblance to the original settlement. Yet, although the old salt kettles have long since disappeared, salt production still remains Grand Saline's principal industry. Morton has two distinct types of production there.

In the center of the town there is the efficient modern salt plant turning out both vacuum pan and grainer salt. The vacuum pans are smaller here than at other plants, but there are two sets going and a substantial output is thus assured.

Manufacturing and refining of evaporated salt and preparing it for sale as table salt, blocks and so on, goes on here in the same manner as at similar plants in other parts of the country.

A mile or so away from the evaporating plant Morton in 1928 opened the Kleer mine. As this is one of the most modern and best equipped salt mines in the world, let's take a fairly detailed look at the mining processes.

From a tall structure known as a "head house" near the refining plant, cables operated by powerful electric motors run the mine hoist and elevator. We take the elevator and drop down slowly into the earth, passing through successive layers of clay, limestone, marl, shale, and other deposits which the changing conditions of the earth's crust have left through the ages.

Through these has been cut a shaft 15 feet in diameter in which our elevator is now descending. Somewhere below us we know is the stratum of pure rock salt. We are well into it at 750 feet down. The elevator stops and we step out into a brilliantly lighted hall of such size one can scarcely believe that the hand of man has created it.

Imagine a wide hall eighty feet high, stretching away with supporting pillars or columns fifty feet in diameter. Walls and ceilings gleam in the light of the incandescents as with jewels like some cave described in The Thousand-and-One-Nights. You walk on a soft carpet of fine salt—or if that has recently been cleared away, on the hard surface of rock salt. The air is pure and invigorating, with the temperature constant throughout the year.

There is a conveyor over there, moving continually from the "working face" (that is, from the point where the salt is actually being dug out of the wall) to the hoist. It brings chunks of all sizes to load into 5-ton hoist cars and go up to the ground level for refining in the plant which we saw out there by the head house. You wonder how this great mine was ever constructed.

Well, here are the steps in opening a rock salt mine: First, find a workable vein of salt. Salt deposits in different parts of the United States vary enormously in thickness. Some places the veins are only a few feet thick—too thin to mine profitably or practically.

Again, you will find veins of sufficient thickness to mine, but interspersed with layers of rock or shale which often makes mining difficult or prohibitive in cost.

Yet again, as in Texas and Louisiana, the salt occurs in great blocks (or domes) and in almost a pure state.

Mining in the thinner workable veins—as in New York, Michigan and Kansas—is very similar to mining coal. Getting salt from

A steady stream of rock salt moves via conveyor belt from the work-ing face in Kleer Mine.

the huge salt domes, in Louisiana, and here in Texas, entails an entirely different procedure, requiring special methods.

In these two states, the first step in opening your mine, is to sink a shaft down into the salt block or dome. There is so much salt in these blocks that you can safely leave a thick "roof" to prevent any possibility of a break-through from the surface, or of surface water seeping into the mine.

Next, you start your "working face" by blasting out a chamber —the salt, of course, being hoisted up and prepared for the market. From this main chamber, galleries are driven out through the salt and "rooms" are excavated—rooms usually about 60 feet wide and often as high as 80 feet. In this excavating, you are careful to leave great supporting salt pillars—about 50 feet square to hold up the roof.

Now as we stand here inside this great high-ceilinged hall, with various hallways and corridors leading out from it, we gain some idea of how much salt has been taken from the Kleer Mine since it was first set going in 1928.

To see how the salt is taken out, we'll walk out to the working face in one of the rooms opening off the main hall. Look! There are some men drilling a series of holes in the face of the wall with electric drills, about six feet above the floor. They'll put dynamite in there and blow out a big new section of salt. Now that salt must have some place to fall when the dynamite jolts it loose from its age-old bed. So here comes a machine which will make a place for it to fall in.

It is a strange looking thing with an extension that looks like a sawfish "bill" sticking out in front. Around this extended bill runs an endless chain with a row of close-set, business-like saw-teeth, whirling at a fast clip. The machine moves in with its motors roaring full tilt, the sawteeth spinning around flat against the floor. Wham! It begins cutting into the bottom of the wall, moving slowly sidewise as those teeth cut out a slit about two inches thick which reaches back some six feet under the salt wall. In a short time the whole of the working face is undercut. (Now, when it is blasted loose, the salt will have somewhere to fall; that's the reason for that slit).

Boom! The dynamite knocks loose many tons of salt from its bed. Down it falls in masses of various sizes. The smoke clears away. Workmen get busy on the pile and load it—big lumps, medium-sized lumps, small lumps, and fine crystals—on the conveyor belt which moves it back to the hoist for its trip up to the open air and refining. For more than a hundred centuries, probably, that salt has lain there in its bed. Only a few minutes are required to dig it out and start it on its long way to become an article of commerce for modern America. The drillers erect staging and start drilling for another blast.

"Upstairs," the salt from the hoist falls over onto iron grids—evenly spaced iron bars—which screen the larger from the smaller lumps. The smaller lumps and the fine crystals follow another course to the mill. The larger lumps, however, go to the crusher which makes them small, dropping them on a belt for their trip through the plant. Since the salt is already dry, it needs no mill drying as does evaporated salt. But here in the plant at the Kleer Mine the same system of screening is employed as that we saw in the Port Huron, Michigan, plant.

Rock salt in many American mines occurs in thick beds, interstratified with various layers of other deposits. For that reason, the product from those mines comes up with many original impurities in it and must go through certain further processes before it is marketable for most purposes.

The salt domes at Grand Saline, Texas, and Weekes Island, La., however, are pure halite.

Having seen the three modern methods by which the American salt industry obtains the salt it supplies us with, let's touch briefly upon the manifold ways in which salt serves us, making many facets of our daily life more worth the living. Salt, as we all know, is vital in our food. But there are many other uses for it—uses about which you have probably never thought. You will discover that as you read the succeeding chapters.

CHAPTER TWENTY-FOUR

A CALENDAR OF SALT CUSTOMS— HERE, THERE AND EVERYWHERE

A N ANCIENT TALE records that a desert robber broke into the palace of an Oriental potentate; but that as he was stealthily departing with his rich loot, he stumbled over a crock of salt in the pantry. Whereupon he threw away the treasure and took the salt instead!

Whether the yarn is true or legendary, it points up one indisputable fact. The ancient Oriental placed an inordinately high value upon a product which today we accept and use as casually as the water that slakes our thirst.

Then as now, salt was necessary to life. And because of that essentiality, it came to be used as a symbol for life; and not only for life itself, but for the most desirable qualities in human personality. A man of particular worth or a person with lively wit or wisdom "had salt," or was "a man of salt."

191

"Scipio omnes sale superbat!" Thus Cicero characterized the great Roman General. (Scipio surpassed everyone in salt.)

"Salt Cleopatra!" So Shakespeare dubbed that brilliant and beautiful Egyptian queen, desired by nearly all men of her day.

In Andalusia where the women grow up lovely with Titian hair and brown eyes, salt is synonymous with grace and charm. You pay your girl a high compliment if you call her your little salt box.

"The salt of the party!" say the Arabs of an especially lively and witty guest; while the grave Orientals shake their heads solemnly over a youth who is none too bright. "He was not salted when he was born," they observe. What they refer to is their native custom of washing and salting a baby immediately after birth. Something, they say, is missing in that boy!—and it may very well be due to the omission of salting.

In the city of Syracuse (not New York, but Sicily) there was once a popular misconception of the meaning of the Latin words *sedes sapientae* in the Laurentian litany. Therefore, just as the old-time American negroes corrupted the words "the very spirit and image" into "the very spittin' image," the ancient Syracusans twisted the prayer phrase into *sale e sapeinza* (salt and wisdom). In Syracuse, salt and wisdom went hand in hand, so they prayed for it!

In some countries, its preservative quality made salt a symbol of incorruptibility. The old Russians put a little salt in the coffins of their dead to signify the incorruptibility of the human spirit. The Scotch people of long ago measured out three handfuls of salt into a plate and placed it on the breast of a corpse. The rite was always performed by one of the oldest ladies in the community. She then arranged three empty dishes on the hearth, close to the fire. All the other attendants in the room went out. Soon they returned walking backwards and repeating in a kind of macabre singsong:

Salt mine exterior and refining plant, Grand Saline, Texas.

This machine undercuts the salt before blasting it loose.

After the blast — large and small lumps of salt.

Spacious halls of a Texas salt mine.

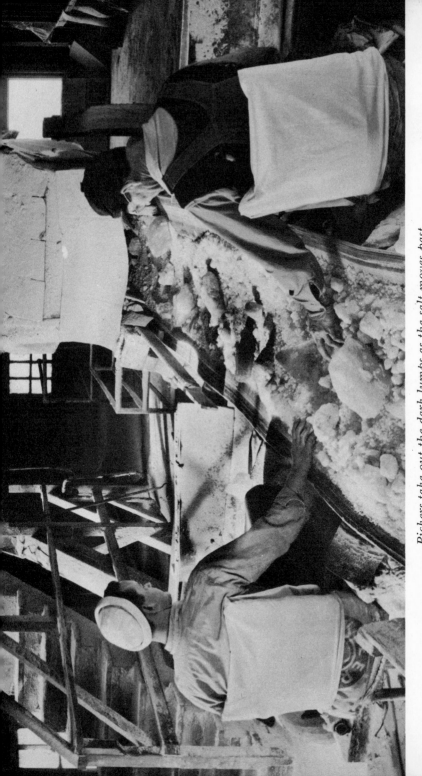

Pickers take out the dark lumps as the salt moves past.

Shaking screens sort the salt according to size.

Salt goes to market by the carload!

Thrice the torchie, thrice the saltie,
Thrice the dishes toom for "loffie" (praise),
These three times three ye must wave round
The corpse until it sleep sound.
Sleep sound and wake nane,
Till to heaven the soul's gane.

Coming down to modern times, this same preservative quality of salt perhaps has caused it to become a symbol of making pledges: a stabilizer of agreements. This symbolism was particularly common in Arabia where salt was highly valued by the desert nomads. Even today when an Arab "swears by the salt," you may be sure that he will keep his word.

Baron du Tott, in his book, *Memoirs of the Turks and Tartars,* tells of visiting with a high-ranking Arab pasha. The pasha, wishing to prove his sincerity, turned briskly "to one of my domestics who followed me: 'Bring me directly,' said he, 'some bread and salt.' Taking a little salt between his fingers and putting it with a mysterious air on a bit of bread, he ate it with a devout gravity, assuring me that I might rely on him." The salt consecrated the pledge.

Members of the fierce Bedouin tribes pledged their agreements by putting salted bread into each other's mouths. "By this salt and bread, I will not betray thee," they chanted meanwhile. So binding is the salt covenant that to add an oath would have been like gilding the lily.

One of the best stories showing the power of salt in human relations is told by the traveler, John Macgregor, in a book called *"The Rob Roy on the Jordan."* Macgregor was travelling through the desert when he was taken prisoner by a band of Arabs. In spite of vigorous remonstrances, they marched him before an old sheik in his dingy desert tent.

Macgregor argued. The sheik bargained. They got nowhere fast. Macgregor had a happy thought. From his pocket he took a box of fine salt and offered some to the old man. The sheik's eyes flew open. Never before had he seen salt so fine and white. In fact, he thought it was sugar and eagerly he put out his hand to taste it. Then his face twisted with the sharp salt flavor and with the knowledge that he had been tricked. Immediately Macgregor put some into his own mouth and laughed aloud as he clapped the old fellow on the back.

"Is it sukker?" asked the sheik with an air of innocence, though he knew full well what it was.

"No—salt!" exclaimed Macgregor. The two had partaken of the substance that men cannot eat together and be enemies. So in a little while Macgregor was released and started on his way with the blessings of the now friendly natives.

Over and over, so it is said, during the Indian Mutiny against the British in 1859, certain of the Sepoy troops were restrained from joining the mutiners: They had "sworn by their salt" to serve the English crown.

Many primitive peoples still consider salt a symbol of blood. In Siam (Thailand), when two men wish to take a pledge of friendship, they drink salted water together, then each takes a lasting vow. This act, they believe, makes them "blood brothers" in spirit. But the use of salt as a substitute for blood is more than a symbol. It has a sound medicinal application. In modern medical practice, when a wounded man cannot be provided with blood transfusion, a weak saline solution is often substituted, salt being a vital blood constituent.

This relationship between salt and blood probably accounts for the use of salt in certain religious sacrifices. Chinese worshippers (Buddhists) add salt to their sacrifices. The ancient Hebrews, also. Herodotus, Greek historian, reports that the Romans burned oil with salt in many of their offerings to the deities. Natives worshipping at little wayside shrines in Central America formerly were wont to offer salt as a sacrifice.

The American Indian, too, considered salt a gift of the deity. Little wonder then that men came to believe it had a power of warding off evil.

A traveler in the Nubian desert once saw some native women in a ceremony meant to protect travellers from evil genii. A caravan was about to set out when the women appeared "with earthen vessels filled with burning coals." As the yellow salt flame leaped up, they chanted in unison:

"May you be blessed in going and in coming!"

The Chinese burn salt, but with them it is a New Year's custom to determine what luck the year at hand will bring. They throw on handfuls at a time. If it burns brightly, a good year is portended.

Many an American woman remembers a foolish school girl Halloween rite. To find out who your life mate will be, boil an egg until it is hard. Cut it open, remove the yolk and fill the cavity with salt. At midnight eat it—all of it! Never mind if it tastes red hot and salty! What's a bit too much salt in determining a question of such romantic importance? Now, without speaking to anyone or taking a single drink of water, go to bed. Before morning, so you must believe, your future mate will appear in a dream offering you a drink of water. This gruelling custom was sometimes observed on the night before May Day.

Nor is that the only way in which salt may be instrumental in affairs of the heart. Here's an old English belief: If a girl will, for three successive nights, throw a bit of salt on the fire, saying the following rhyme, she will bring back the interest of a straying boy friend:

> It is not this salt I wish to burn,
> It is my lover's heart to turn;
> May he neither rest nor happy be
> Until he comes and speaks to me.

Salt has a place, too, at weddings. At a wedding breakfast in Pomerania, a servant always carries around a plate of it at the end of a meal. Each guest takes a pinch and places a piece of money on the plate, but whether the money goes to the servant as a gratuity or to the happy couple as a gift, deponent sayeth not. A wedding in the Canton of Bern, Switzerland, often sees the groom go forth fortified with a piece of bread in one pocket, some salt in another and the Geneva Psalter in his hand. Now he is safe from all ills.

Then after the wedding, because salt and bread represent the first necessities of bodily existence, these are the first articles taken into the house of a newly-married pair.

Salt customs, however, do not stop with the courtship or the wedding. In the Pyrennes country—notably the Basqueland— you had better carry a few pinches of the Great Savorer in your left vest pocket if you wish to have children! For the same reason a German bride carries salt in her slipper.

A Scotch couple strews salt over the new home the night before the wedding. That not only brings children, all other things being equal, but keeps away witches. And its efficacy can be proved! I once asked John McDonald, of Washington, D. C., late of Aberdeen, Scotland, if it were so.

" 'Tis true, laddie," he replied. "I ken it weel. I carrit salt and strewed it on the ingle and in the bedroom. Janet and I hae six bairns and ne'er a witch hae we seen." For what better proof could you ask?

When the Russian Grand Duke Alexis visited Washington in 1872, the wife of the Russian Minister to the United States presented him with a silver platter. On the platter was a loaf of black bread and in the bread was imbedded a golden salt cellar. An old Slavic custom, you see, favored the gift of salt to a visiting potentate.

Once, years ago, in a gypsy camp in Roumania, one of the men lost a packet of money.

"I can't find it!" he lamented to the chief of the tribe. "Have cheer, my son," the old man answered. "I'll do all possible to recover your treasure." And this is what he did.

He fastened two sticks in the form of a cross, putting at the top a piece of bread sprinkled with salt. Then he called all members of the tribe to one place. Each one he made to pass before the symbol and take an oath upon it that he had not stolen the money.

One by one they came. One by one they took the oath and retired. At last an old woman hobbled up. She stretched forth her claw-like hand as the others had done to make her oath. Then she faltered, turned pale. Snatching back her hand, she thrust it into her voluminous skirt, drew out the stolen gold, and flung it down.

For her punishment, so the story goes, she was beaten and thrown out of camp; and she knew she risked just that for stealing. But she dared not swear to a lie on those two sacred symbols—the cross and salt.

In Sumatra the most solemn oath of a tribe is: "May my harvest fail, my cattle die, and may I never taste salt again if I do not speak truth."

To the native of Morocco, salt is a talisman against evil; and he always carries a bit with him.

Having anciently so great a value, it is hardly surprising that superstition grew up concerning the spilling of salt. Didn't Grandmother throw a pinch over her shoulder to ward off bad luck when she spilled it? In some of the copies of Leonardo da Vinci's painting, the Last Supper, you'll notice an overturned salt cellar beside the plate of Judas Iscariot to signify that he had incurred the anger of heaven.

"The sacredness and dignity of salt!" exclaims Jean de Marcounille in his treatise on the subject, published in Paris, 1584. "This mineral is like unto the four elements—earth, air, fire, and water. So universal, so necessary to life, it is the *fifth element.*"

Salt in Holy Writ

The Bible contains more than a score of references to salt. You recollect what happened to Lot's wife, fleeing from the heaven-destroyed cities of the plain? Arabian guides in Palestine today point out a high chalk pile, gully-washed from the cliffs near the Dead Sea, and explain to you that it is Lot's wife—the lady who looked back, centuries ago, to her own undoing. Scientists, however, remain a little on the skeptical side.

An old Jewish tradition seeks to give the reason for this woman's salty "translation." She became salt, says the legend, because she betrayed the presence of the two angels who had come to Lot's home the evening before the family's flight, to warn them of impending doom. She had gone to some neighbors with the very normal request:

"Give me some salt, for we have guests." And by that the men of Sodom knew the strangers were there and demanded that they be delivered up. Therefore, Lot's wife was turned to salt as a fitting retribution—a sort of punishment-fit-the-crime justice.

Salt was used for two widely different reasons in the Holy Land. The people needed it as a food, of course, and they had to have it for use in their religious ceremonies. It had an important part in the domestic economy of the day—preserver of fish, of olives, and of hides: three ways in which we use it today. Further, the Palestinians employed it as a medicine. A grain of salt in a decayed tooth was supposed to effect a cure—to stop the ache at least. Bread and olives dipped in salt made up the poor man's daily fare.

Where did their salt come from? From the Dead Sea, naturally. Here, 1,300 feet below the level of the Mediterranean Sea, there was salt for all. The Dead Sea is so full of salt that one can pick up crystals along the shore on almost any day. The Romans who then controlled Palestine had their own salt pits, and placed a tax on all which they supplied. To the Hebrews this sea was not the Dead Sea but the Salt Sea; it gave them the Great Seasoner. The Greeks coined the name "Dead Sea" for the very obvious reason that there was no animal or vegetable life in it.

An enormous amount of salt went into the religious rites of the Jewish people. Indeed salt accompanied every sacrifice under the Jewish dispensation. "And every oblation of thy meal-offering shalt thou season with salt...with all thine oblations thou shalt offer salt." So reads Leviticus 2:13. That meant, of course, that large quantities must be kept on hand for use in the Temple. Worshippers could thus obtain what they required in the Temple market. In preparing burnt offerings, salt was rubbed on the flesh of the killed animals which served to deplete it of blood; this rite alone demanded a great deal of salt.

Salt in another act of worship is recorded in Ezekiel 43:24, "And thou shalt bring them before Jehovah and the priests shall pour salt upon them."

To the devout Jews, therefore, salt had the property of preserving from corruption; it could be regarded as ritually pure. More than that, say some authorities, in the old Assyrian language the word *tabtu* (salt) and another word *tabtu* (blessing) have the same ideogram and are written exactly alike.

Covenants were very solemn agreements in both the Old and New Testaments, and breaking of a covenant was a most serious offense. To violate a covenant with the Lord God was the grossest possible evil, followed inevitably by severest punishment. In Genesis, 17:14, we find "that soul shall be cut off from his people; he hath broken my covenant." Deuteronomy 17:2 says ". . . man and woman that doeth that which is evil in the sight of Jehovah Thy God in transgressing his covenant. . .thou shalt stone them to death with stones." Other punishments for breaking covenants were being burnt with fire, carried away into slavery, brought into the pit of destruction, or given into the hands of them that might seek one's life.

Now of all the sacred covenants, the "Covenant of Salt" was considered the most binding. The term implied permanency, purity, steadfastness, unchangeableness. Three times is the Covenant of Salt mentioned in the Old Testament. Chronicles 12:5 indicates there was both a sacred and national implication: "Ought ye not to know that Jehovah the God of Israel gave the kingdom of Israel to David forever, even to him and to his son, by a Covenant of Salt?"

Again, the Lord makes a Covenant of Salt with Aaron and his

son. "All of the heave offerings of the Holy things, which the children of Israel offer unto the Lord, have I given thee, and thy sons and daughters with thee, as a due forever; it is a Covenant of Salt forever before the Lord unto thee and to thy seed with thee."

Through Moses, God enjoins the people of Israel to be faithful in their sacrificial offerings at the altar. "Neither shalt thou suffer the Salt of the Covenant to be lacking from the meal-offering." (Leviticus 2:13.)

In another way the mystical binding quality of salt is indicated. Twice in the Old Testament certain groups protested against receiving salt from a foreign ruler since that obligated them to be faithful to him. In Ezra 4:14 the adversaries of Judah and Benjamin protest: "Now because we eat the salt of the palace we are bound by a covenant, and it is not meet for us to see the king's dishonor; therefore have we sent and certified the king."

Further on in the same book we read of King Darius giving the Jews a supply of things needed for their sacrifices in their own country, in return for their services. Among the items were salt, wine, and oil. Wise old King Darius ordained that they receive salt *without prescribing how much*. He knew the Jews' belief that the more salt they took from him, the more firmly they were bound to him.

There is also a reverse side to salt lore—it becomes a symbol of death and destruction. We all know that too much salt destroys vegetation. Abimilech "slew the people of Shechem and sowed it with salt" according to Judges 9:45.* Moses warned the Israelites in Deuteronomy 29:23 that the land of the disobedient "is brimstone, and salt, and a burning." God warns in Jeremiah 17:6 that the man whose heart departed from Jehovah "shall inhabit the parched places in the wilderness, a salt land."

---

*In the American Civil War, General Halleck, Federal Chief of Staff, advised General Sherman, after the burning of Charleston, South Carolina, to sow the site with salt. Sherman, however, did not comply.

Again, wisdom and a pleasant speech was typified by salt. "Let your speech be always with grace, seasoned with salt, that you may know how to answer each other," St. Paul wrote to the Colossians.

The Jews of Christ's day rubbed new-born children with salt—probably as a sign that they were purified and dedicated to God. The Prophet Ezekiel says poetically of the wayward city of Jerusalem, ". . . thou wast not salted at all, nor swaddled at all. No eye pitieth thee to do any of these things unto thee."

The custom, in revised form, probably, survives in the Roman Catholic Church today: salt is placed on the tongue at baptism. It is also a constituent of the holy water sprinkled on the congregation before the Sunday morning mass.

Salt entered the conversation of men in biblical times just as it does today. "When the salt hath lost its savor." These words may have referred to salt so impure that it retained little of the salty taste. St. James (3:12) asked, "Can a fig tree yield olives or a vine tree figs? Neither can salt water yield sweet." Job, the afflicted patriarch, demands, "Can that which hath no savor be eaten without salt?" One Greater than Job, seeking for a standard by which to dignify human personality, said to his followers: "Ye are the salt of the earth."

The Valley of Salt, mentioned at least half a dozen times in the Bible, is thought beyond all doubt to mean the valley in which the Dead Sea lies, especially that part identified with the southern end of it and called in Hebrew "Ham-melah."

A City of Salt is mentioned as one of the six cities of Judah "in the wilderness"; but no one is quite sure to what city the reference is made. It may have been the seat of an ancient salt trade.

In Ezekiel 47:11, in the prophet's description of the ideal future, we find that after the Dead Sea has been sweetened as a whole, the marshes are still reserved for salt making.

And finally, salt served Elisha the Prophet in performing a great miracle. It is described in 2 Kings 2:20.

"And the men of the city said unto Elisha, Behold, we pray thee, the situation of this city is pleasant, as my lord seeth; but the water is bad, and the land miscarrieth. And he said, Bring me a new cruse. And they brought it to him and he put salt therein. And he went forth unto the spring of the waters and cast the salt therein, and said: Thus saith Jehovah, I have healed these waters; there shall not be from thence any more death or miscarrying. So the waters were healed unto this day, according to the word of Elisha which he spake."

* * * *

CHAPTER TWENTY-FIVE

SEASONER AND PRESERVER

A GOOD BRINE," our grandmothers said, "will keep anything."

There was considerable truth in the statement. A good brine or some other form of salt has been man's chief food preservative ever since he stopped eating raw flesh and began to augment his diet with grain and vegetables. You could well say, indeed, that salt is a symbol of man's transition from the nomadic stage of existence to the agricultural.

Long ago, when man's food consisted almost entirely of raw meat, he killed each meal with a stone or club or clumsy spear and ate it as soon as it was "bled." It remained good a day, a week, or possibly longer, depending on the state of the weather. But did he worry about that? Not our paleolithic ancestor! The woods were full of meals. A man with a good spear or club, or maybe a trap, could refill the larder in no time at all.

Which was good as far as it went. But gradually, as the human family increased, there were more mouths to feed. As more and more animals fell under the stone axe, meat grew scarcer. So, to insure himself a supply of food, man had to shift his residence, seeking new animals to kill. That was why the early human family was nomadic—moving from place to place; moving endlessly, again and yet again. It was a great nuisance. But what else was there to do? One had to eat.

Time moved right along and man (and his wife) discovered some important facts about food. In winter food would keep— stay good for months even. In warmer weather, if you put the next day's meat in the farthest, coolest corner of the cave, it didn't acquire that unpleasant smell and taste as quickly as meat left where it was warm. But in time even food kept cool would become putrid.

Once when her husband had had a particularly good day in the woods, the wife hung the meat all around the cave. Some of it happened to be near the fire; and she noticed then that it dried and shrivelled, but remained edible for an even longer time than cold raw meat. After that she made a practice of shredding some meat thin and drying it near the blaze. The smoke rolled up and about the meat and left a sharp mellow taste where it touched.

We know that all primitive peoples preserved foods. The American Indians were drying and curing their "pemican" long before Columbus showed up. Smoking and drying meat, and burying other foods are still used as methods of preservation.

Today we smoke meat not only to preserve it but to give it a distinctive flavor.

Gradually as the human family found animal flesh harder to procure, men began to ask: "How are we going to make our meat supply last longer?" That led them to piece out their diet by eating berries, root and leaf vegetables, and cereal grasses— thereby unwittingly advancing their health. But they kept on looking for something to make the meat which spoiled taste better.

After a long time, man found that salt did just that. Spread over a piece of meat, salt warded off decay and the vile smell that decaying meats acquire. Most people don't realize that it was not until the era of industrial development and the scientific research that accompanied it in the 19th century, that man actually learned *why* his food spoiled.

For centuries no one knew as we now know that micro-organisms were the real cause of most food spoilage; they simply knew that some mysterious form of decay soon set in and deprived them of the use of their food.

Finding that salt was a preservative not only gave man a better supply of food that would keep for a longer period, but it had a definite impact upon history and the status of nations. Salted meat provided food for ships' crews on long voyages and for armies marching long distances from country to country. Of course ships' meat had to be so heavily salted that it was necessary to soak out some of the brine in fresh water before using it.

"Lay late," confided the famous Samuel Pepys to his equally famous diary in the 17th century, "and to dine with Lady A. off Berkeley Square. The roast did smell so vile that Sir Joshua was fain to leave the table. Lady A. had it removed. We dined but scantily. And so to bed."

What happens when you salt meat? Meat absorbs the salt by means of its moisture content and the salt is quickly carried by these natural juices through the fibre of the food. This protects it from the micro-organisms that make it spoil.

There was a time before modern refrigeration came into use that salt was used to cure practically all kinds of meat, domestic or wild.

When the farmer learned to cure his meat, he could butcher early in the season—even in warm weather if need be—because he could store his extra meat or haul it to the nearest town and sell it profitably.

American colonists early discovered the preservative value of salt and they used it in curing meat, fish, and butter.

"Most of our people are sorely dependent on salt." So writes a gentleman in Leesburg, Va., within a stone's throw of the present Capital of the Nation, in 1776. "Hot weather makes it impossible to keep meat fresh longer than one day. The only animals that may be killed without loss are young hogs and fowls. When we have the salt, we cure meat this way: Keep it in salt water from ten to fourteen days. Then rub it with salt and smoke it in the smokehouse for several weeks."

One farmer kept pieces of beefsteak weighing from three to five pounds in brine for a week. Next he placed them from five to six feet above the fire and left them there for two or three weeks. After that he could store them safely.

Meat, still one of man's chief foods, is still cured by salt. American packing houses use thousands of tons annually. For larger pieces—hams, bacon, sides, and shoulders—a specially prepared brine is pumped along the bones into the meat. This starts the cure on the inside while another salt preparation is rubbed on the outside. For smaller pieces, the usual method used is the brine cure—soaking in a salt solution, just as grandma recommended. A special salt product is used to season and preserve sausages—once, (actually!) called the poor man's meat, but no longer.

As mentioned previously, we Americans like our butter salted. The article known as "sweet butter" (unsalted) has never become popular on this side of the Atlantic. Experiments testing the preservative powers of salt in butter disclose that in the first 30 days yeast mold and bacteria increase very rapidly in sweet butter—with only a slight increase in mold, and an actual *decrease* in yeast and bacteria in the salted article. The same conditions apply to oleomargerine.

Not only meat and butter, but any food with a high water content can be preserved by salt. Many foods, however—fruits for example—wouldn't taste good if we used salt as the preserver. In foods like meat, fish, and butter, the salt, moistened by the water in the food, spreads out through the fibers very quickly by a process known as osmosis. This keeps micro-organisms from developing. Not only that, some insects and many other pests steer clear of salted food.

The human family has been eating fish time out of mind. The world's fishing history has been well sprinkled with salt. Since fish decomposes even more quickly than meat, salt has always been wanted in places where the fishing industry flourished. Some historians say that salt was the first and principal cargo of those early exponents of foreign trade, the Phoenicians. They took salt from the Spanish deposits 2,000 miles distant, and from the Palestinian ports near the Dead Sea. The Mediterranean cities proved excellent markets for salt.

When in the course of time the Roman Catholic Church prescribed a fish diet for a considerable part of the year, a new demand for salt was at once created.

For years the history of New England was dominated by the fish industry and its satellite, the salt industry. English fishing interests in the New World colonies once had a fleet of 250 ships. That was in the 17th century. Since salt was then scarce in England, the British Government agreed to protect the Portuguese (who had plenty) from their rivals, the French, provided they (the Portuguese) would furnish salt for England's American fish trade. Once, at least, the Portuguese reneged on their bargain. In 1678 Lord Parkhurst moved in Commons to recover from the Portuguese as much fish "as 600 livres salt would preserve." They had failed to deliver the salt—and that brought about a spoilage of just that much fish.

With her accustomed trade acumen, Britain decreed in 1663 that all commodities sent to her American colonists must be loaded and shipped from English ports. This law—a maneuver, of course, to force the colonies to get their imports from England—was a thorn in the side of the Americans.

"If we send our fish to Bilboa, Spain," they complained, "at great hazard and procure fruits, oil, soap, wine, and salt, (the bulk of loadings being salt because that is most necessary for us and always to be had at Cadiz) we must go to England to pay his Majesty's customs; which is as the cutting off of our hands and feet to our trade, and this orphan plantation (New England) will be crushed."

European nations with ample salt—notably Portugal and France—engaged in the Newfoundland fishing industry. That brought to America many ancestors of the present large French population of the Gaspé Peninsula in eastern Canada. Little wonder that America's first industry was the manufacture of salt!

Coming down to modern times, commercial fisheries still use enormous quantities of salt. As soon as caught, the fish are rushed into refrigerator containers; split open, cleaned, and washed. They are then salted and packed in large barrels and left to cure. Salting is an exact science. The modern fishery employs a salometer to gauge just the right cure. Salt for fish must be of high purity. Fillets, for instance, may be kept in storage three months longer if a pure salt is used.

The crews of old-time sailing vessels ate rather prodigious quantities of sauerkraut and pickles. This was about the only way they could get green vegetables into their diet to prevent constipation and scurvy. It was also one way Grandma managed to get green vegetables into Grandpa and the family in seasons when none grew in the garden.

Sauerkraut has been a winter standby for many hundreds of years all over the earth. The Chinese made something quite similar long before the birth of Christ. About all that is necessary for a good crock of kraut is shredded cabbage and about $2\frac{1}{2}$ percent of its weight in salt. The salt draws water from the cabbage and starts fermentation. Now with a heavyish weight on top of the cabbage, in not very long at all you'll have the makings of a really good dinner. The salt has brought about the change. It has exchanged some of the water in the cabbage (in the cucumber, if it is pickles) for brine. Brine controls the bacteria, eliminating those that would cause spoiling. It also preserves the chlorophyl and other insoluble content.

Pickles and olives are treated in much the same fashion, i.e., they are put in a good stiff brine; vinegar and spices are often added. The olive most commonly "pickled" in this country is the Mission olive grown in California. Brought to the factory as soon as they are picked, they are either pickled at once or stored in brine.

During the last war, many a housewife preserved the foods from her victory garden by salting them away. She alternated layers of salt and vegetables in much the fashion sauerkraut is made. The brine thus formed kept the vegetables intact; and a soaking in fresh water made them ready to eat.

In old-time drug stores—the kind with the big, beautiful jars of colored water in the windows—you saw baskets full of little packets labelled *Canning Powders*. Filled with preservatives such as borax, soda, formaldehyde, and benzoic acid, they really preserved foods and did it well. The only trouble was that if these substances were taken in large enough quantities, they were bound to be harmful to the ultimate consumer.

Neither Grandma nor the old-time canning factory used enough to do much harm. Still there was the possibility of harm, and their use was outlawed in our country by the Pure Food Laws of 1907 and later years.

Now common salt is just as much a chemical as any of these outlaws. The big difference is that it isn't harmful. Improved canning methods have overcome many of the former difficulties of preserving foods; but salt is still one of the best and most frequently used preservatives in the home and in the cannery.

Salt helps, too, in dehydrating vegetables. A hot salt-water bath before drying loosens the skins and provides a protective coating.

If all the miles of all the shelves of canned goods in grocery stores were placed end to end around the world, they would form a fitting tribute to a little French confectioner, by name Nicholas Appert.

Back in the 1790's Appert began experimenting with cooking and preserving in the little kitchen behind his shop near Paris.

Encouraged later by Napoleon, who realized the vast advantages such preserved food would give him in his military operations, Appert worked away with kettles and bottles and corks—cooking food, putting it in bottles, wiring in the corks to prevent their popping out, and putting the bottles into cloth sacks which he lowered into kettles to cook some more. Though he never knew anything about bacteria, he did discover that spoilage is caused by air; and after fifteen years of work, he presented to the French Government a little book called *The Book for All Households or The Art of Preserving Animal and Vegetable Substances for Many Years.*

On that little book are based, with some variations, the world-wide industrial canning processes of today!

The salt necessary in canning vegetables, fish, and meats is provided now by salt tablets. Manufactured in sizes suitable for the various sized cans of the different foods, they are automatically dropped into each can just before it is sealed. They both season and preserve.

"Salt is good," said St. Mark. It's certainly good as a food preserver.

CHAPTER TWENTY-SIX

A PURPOSE FOR EVERY SALT—
A SALT FOR EVERY PURPOSE

ALL OF MAN'S FOOD is supplied by Nature from her plant or animal kingdom—except salt. Since the animals get their food from plants or from other plant-eating animals on which they feed, the whole process goes finally back to plants. Through the mysterious processes of plant life we obtain all the necessary sugars, starches, proteins, and vitamins that spell health—all, that is, except salt. That, man himself must add.

Long ago a wise statesman, Thomas Jefferson, said, "Salt is a necessary of life." Let's see what modern science has to say on this subject. Doctor Morris Fishbein, of the American Medical Association, is on record that sodium chloride is more important to the body's well-being than any other of the chemical salts in the human makeup. Experiments were made not long ago with rabbits to find what happens when all salt is extracted from animal food. The first few days these rabbits were without salt, they became nervous and irritable. Even a rabbit gets riled if you withhold his salt from him! Next, a pronounced weakness manifested itself. Later, they became completely paralyzed and, in a short while, died.*

The same experiment was then tried out on human beings. In the first few days they showed little change. By the fifth day the patients were perspiring unduly and losing their appetites. Increasingly they showed signs of discomfort—muscular soreness and twitching by the end of the eighth day. Experiments had to stop there. Men aren't rabbits. Even in a good cause science does not dare to deny salt to the human machine for any lengthy period. Permanent disability or death might result. Jefferson was right.*

Salt has long been recognized as an essential element and as such has its important place in human diet. Because of differences in climate and soil, man's food varies greatly in different continents and in different sections of different continents. Yet from Chile to Tibet, from New York to Australia, man must have salt in some form if he is to remain alive and keep healthy. The Chinese and certain religious groups of India eat little meat; yet they must add salt to their diet. The North American Indian ate heavily of meat; yet even they needed salt and procured it from the natural salt springs, from the sea or from the Great Salt Lake to which, long ago, they made ceremonious treks to visit the old "Witch Salt Woman" who they believed lived there.

Nobody is ever quite sure just how many elements make up this vast earth; every once in so often a new element is discovered. But there are about seventeen elements that are known to be essential to life. They are sodium, chlorine, carbon, hydrogen, oxygen, nitrogen, sulphur, calcium, magnesium, phosphorous, potassium, manganese, copper, cobalt, iron, zinc, and iodine.

---

*From: "The Ethnology of Salt in Aboriginal North America," by Helen Virginia Hunter, University of Pennsylvania, 1940.

A pronounced lack in any of these spells disaster to human well-being. Fortunately, with the exception of common salt, all of them are usually found in sufficient quantity in the plants used for food. But, to repeat, Nature has left it to man to supply his own salt.

Salt is so important to man because it is a constituent of many parts of the body—especially the blood, the lymph, the digestive juices. In the blood stream salt furthers good circulation and heart action. In the gastric juices it aids in the manufacture of the hydrochloric acid necessary to the digestion of proteins in the stomach. It steps up the production of bile, which stimulates digestion in the intestines. Salt stimulates, too, the peristaltic movement of the digestive tract, and affects to a certain extent the elasticity of the muscles. That isn't all. It aids in growth, regulates the water content of the various body tissues, and has a part to play in respiration. Thus, it's not hard to see why salt (or one of its components, or the combination of one of its components with other elements) is essential to our well-being.

Why is salt liked by both man and beast? Because in the fine fitness of nature's processes healthy animals, two-footed or four-footed, nearly always like, and even crave, the foods they most need. That is only animal instinct. Watch a small baby tasting salt and you will see him reach for more even while his small mouth is still puckering with the sharp flavor of too much. Moreover, as a general thing, the amount of salt desired is exactly related to the amount required. Long ago we began to put salt on the table within everybody's reach; free choice for all diners! No two persons need exactly the same amount. Wise farmers put salt, loose or in blocks, where their stock can reach it at will.

Salt with iodine added supplies two of the elements necessary to life. Since salt is used by everybody for seasoning and as a food ingredient and, as such, is never used in large quantities, medical authorities agree that salt treated with minute quantities of iodine is an excellent and safe way of supplying this possibly serious lack.

But not only is salt a "necessary of life," it is man's chief appetizer. Can you imagine eating bread made without salt? Or unsalted meat? Or potatoes?

We Americans consume more bread per person than any other nation. All the world loves a baker, or at any rate, the good bread and rolls which he bakes. Good flour, good yeast, good salt, good water—add them up properly and you have the staff of life. Now, the salt in bread is more than a mere flavoring agent. It does three distinct and important things besides adding taste. It helps control the fermentation that takes place in baking. It gives the dough a better texture. It produces a browner crust. Naturally, then, bakers are most particular about the salt they buy. Mother baking bread at home wants the high-grade table salt. Commercial bakers, however, want a dozen different forms of good salt according to the type of bread or pastry for which the salt is used.

Some bakers need a fine fluffy salt to be used in prepared flour— one that will not sink to the bottom when the flour is mixed. Some must have a coarser salt; some a product with a filler; and so on. There is a salt to meet every baker's need.

And butter, too—that very necessary adjunct to good bread and ingredient for many cooked foods! Americans demand good butter, containing just the right amount of salt to please the finicky palate. Butter in the making, therefore, must first be judged by experts known as scorers before being released from the factory.

Scoring butter is usually done the day after the butter is made. It's an interesting sight to watch a scorer judge a piece of butter. First, he takes some on his "butter tryer" and tests it for odor. This is more important than you might think. For instance, the odor of garlic may be there, if the cows have eaten some wild garlic in the fields. Or other foreign odors may have crept in from other sources. The scorer passes the sample under his nose several times to whiff its aroma. If it be good he gives it a clear mark for odor. Next, he tastes it with extreme care. Enough salt?

Too salty? Fresh? Good flavor? So he puts down a mark for taste.

Now he takes up a plug of butter again and examines it intently for body and texture. He must look for such qualities as leakiness, crumbliness, stickiness, flabbiness. All these count in the evaluation of the batch. Next, he judges for color. The final test shows whether there is any undissolved salt present.

Europeans often take their butter unsalted. But Americans, the butter scorer knows, want the full flavor of the bread *and* the spread. And there must be no grittiness. The final score for top grade butter, on the basis of 100 as perfect, must be not less than 91; for first grade, 88; for second grade, 82; for third grade, 75.

Butter salt must be dry so that it will not cake; it must dissolve easily and be of the highest purity. In making oleomargarine, salt is used in about the same quantities and by the same methods as for butter-making.

Another dairy product requiring good salt is cheese. Always a standby in Europe (Hollanders eat it even for breakfast), cheese has become one of the most popular American foods. It is made from cow's milk, goat's milk, or ewe's milk, depending largely on the country or district. The proportion of fat and casein in the milk determines the kind and quality of cheese made from that milk.

Cheese making generally consists of three steps: ripening, curd-making, and aging. Some products such as cottage or cream cheese need no aging. They are eaten fresh.

In making cheese, the aim is to obtain a particular acidity so that with the adding of a curdling agent, a curd will be formed in two or three hours. In making cheddar, a "starter" is first added in case there is not enough natural bacteria in the milk to start the milk curdling. The starter brings about the ripening. Next goes in the curdling agent; rennet, usually, from the lining of a calf's stomach. Soon the mixture solidifies to a mass of curd. It is cut or broken up to allow the whey (water) to escape, and then the mixture is "cooked" or heated and more of the whey removed. Now the curd is cut into strips. The arrangement of the strips is changed continually so that all sides will be exposed to the air.

Salt must now be added to help remove the whey, thus furthering the hardening of the curd. Salt also prevents undesirable forms of fermentation and gives more flavor. Now the curd is ready to put into the hoops for pressing to cement the pieces of curd into a smooth, solid mass and give it the familiar cheese shape.

Macaroni and spaghetti are made from a flour-and-water paste called semoline. Salt, the only constituent in it with any taste, often equals as much as $1\frac{1}{2}$ to $2\frac{1}{2}$ percent. It is added to the dough in the form of brine. Machines press out the excess water, and mold the dough into cords or tubes, after which it is dried by hot air.

Everybody likes salted nuts; so much so that the production of salted peanuts alone has become an important industry. Nut meats are blanched, cooked in deep fat, and then sprinkled with a special type of salt and drained. Nut salt is so fine is can hardly be seen when the meats are wet, but on drying a coating of crystals becomes visible.

A special salt is available not only for every food, but in one case, at least, to satisfy religious scruples. Orthodox Jewish people must have a special type produced under the supervision of Jewish rabbis who certify that Kosher regulations have been complied with. . . . This custom probably originated when it became known that some saltmakers used fat pork to "cut the grain" of the salt—a practice long since discontinued.

Did you know that salt is used in candy making? Yes, the salt tones down the natural bitterness of chocolate and acts as a stabilizing element. It helps to bring out the bland, sweet flavor desirable in good candy. A salt is produced specially for candy manufacturers, and one for popcorn makers.

As was pointed out in a former chapter, salt has been man's chief preserver of food through the ages. As brine, it is also used as a coolant in the making of artificial ice, man's modern food preserver, as well as a melting agent to accelerate the cooling effect of an ice pack, as in a refrigerator car.

Remember that the "fifth element" is not only a food in itself and a preserver of food—it is also a *grower* of food. Today, scientists are trying to find out more about the value of salt as a fertilizer. Salt has a particular relation to soil. Some hundred years ago Horace Greeley (adviser of young men to "go West") wrote: "If five bushels per acre of salt be applied to a field, and it does not thereupon yield five bushels more per acre per annum of corn, I will agree to eat the field!"

Modern agriculturists don't agree that salt improves corn much; but they insist that it improves the quality and yield of certain other crops—beets, swiss chard, celery, turnips, cabbage, radishes, and kale. Too much salt, of course, will kill a tree; but a proper application of it will promote tree growth, tending to produce large, thick leaves and rapid branch growth. There are several types suitable for this use.

Salt has the amazing quality of not only promoting growth of certain needed crops, but it is used to discourage and even kill weeds, particularly the vicious bindweed.

In the U. S. Department of Agriculture's "Handbook for Better Feeding of Livestock" you will find these words: "Don't forget to salt all animals regularly." Animals need salt for the same reasons people need it; there is hardly a body process which does not depend, directly or indirectly, upon salt. You can tell when animals are starving for salt by their behavior. Salt-starved stock will lick *anything* touched by sweaty human hands to get the salt taste. They will chew the wood of their stalls or barn walls for the slight salt flavor that remains there.

A dairy herd experimentally deprived of salt fell off in milk production. They developed "stary" hides, lost their appetites and their bright eyes. And at calving time, their young were either weaklings or still-born. Two groups of swine were fed identical rations—except that one group had no salt. The hogs with free choice of salt put on 96.5% more weight in the same feeding period. With sheep, a diet lacking in salt decreases the wool yield and reduces the number of lambs born.

Farmers salt their hay by adding approximately 20 pounds of salt to each ton. They salt their silage (grass and fodder, stored in silos) as it goes into the cutter. Farm salt is also sulphurized and iodized; animals, too, get goiters with improper diet.

Man can't do much about the weather. But he can do something about its effect on him. Researchers know now that heat exhaustion is caused primarily by the loss of salt in perspiration. Salt tablets are the answer. Billions of salt tablets helped ease the heat for our soldiers and sailors serving in the hot tropical countries, just as they now enable laborers in industry, as well as office workers, to work better and more comfortably in the hottest months of summer.

Curing hides demands salt. Animal skins to be used for leather are completely covered with salt and piled one on top of the other. You've sometimes seen a hole or defect in a shoe or leather coat? That piece of leather was perhaps not thoroughly covered with salt. Curing takes from ten days to two months, depending on the animal from which the hide comes.

Salt is used to glaze pottery, to de-ice roads, to soften water. Brine regenerates, as well as cleans, the Zeolite beds through which hard water flows in the softening process. In soap factories, salt is added to boiling soap to help the soap to "grain" or solidify. Cloth manufacturers, as well as housewives, know that salt sets color in fabrics. It is also used by them as a filler.

In winter time snow and rain will often freeze solid coal moving in open freight cars. Many coal companies, therefore, add salt to their coal while loading. The rain turns the salt to brine and prevents hard freezing. In the oil industry, salt is used to "set" the mud when the rotary bit is driving through rock. A soft place would let the bit slip; but mud mixed with salt helps the situation. Salt also is used on streets and railway switches to melt ice and snow.

The Great Seasoner plays an important part in metallurgy, too, especially in working with copper and zinc. To concentrate the ore, a leaching process (washing away of unwanted particles) is employed. The ore is treated with solutions of sulphuric acid and common salt. This aids the breaking up of the mineral.

In addition, salt is the basis of a large number of chemicals invaluable to modern industry, no less than to modern warfare— high octane gasoline, resins, neoprene rubber, pharmaceuticals, aviation parts, war tanks, explosives, and hundreds of other products. It plays a part in electroplating, photography, glass making and almost every industry you can think of.

Servant in the House

And while we are on the general subject of salt for many purposes, let's enumerate some of the everyday, convenient household ways in which it serves the American family.

As of course you know, salt ranks high as a purifier. Salt water makes an effective gargle, eye-wash, cleanser of open wounds, a before-breakfast drink to relieve constipation, a mouth wash and a dentifrice.

Salt rubs relieve nervous body tension

Iodized salt is a goiter preventative.

Mixed with mustard, salt becomes an effective emetic.

Rubbing damp salt on burns, insect stings, itching places, rashes or hives, smarts like the very devil for a short while, but draws out the soreness.

Salt added to the water in your bath tub gives you the same effect as a dip in the ocean: it relieves fatigue, invigorates, and soothes.

Salt water makes a comforting bath for tired and aching feet.

The well-known, annoying body odor can be greatly reduced, if not entirely eliminated, by frequent applications of salt water.

In the kitchen, salt does a great many things, many of which you most likely never suspected. Skipping the very obvious fact that it goes into practically all foods that require seasoning, salt can perform numerous services that shorten kitchen processes, prevent annoying mishaps and delays; in short, prove an excellent all-around handmaid to the busy housewife. To wit:

Mixing a little salt water with flour, in making cream gravies and soups, keeps lumps from forming.

To make a jelly stiffen quickly, add salt with soda to the bowl of water in which you place the jelly mould to cool.

You save sugar by adding a little salt to cranberry or apple-sauce.

A dish of butter may be kept firm, without ice, by wrapping around it a cloth wrung out of salt water.

Fresh meats and foods can be preserved temporarily by covering them with salt until ready for the icebox or for eating.

Soaking nuts over night in salt water makes it easy to remove the nutmeats whole.

Food cooks faster in a double boiler if you put salt water in the outside container.

To prevent a frying pan from splashing grease, sprinkle a little salt in it.

Put some salt under the bottom of baking tins in the oven to keep them from scorching.

Hot puddings cool quickly by setting the containers in salt water.

A little salt added to parsley makes it chop more easily.

Fresh milk keeps sweet longer when a pinch of salt is added.

To remove that "muddy" taste from fish caught in small streams, wash them in a strong, cold brine.

In cooking fish cakes, you can keep them from sticking by sprinkling a little salt on the skillet before frying.

If you find it hard to handle a slippery fish, dip your fingers first in water, then in salt. Your job will be easier.

Adding salt to eggs makes them beat quickly.

Salting the water in which eggs are poached makes the whites "set."

Add salt to water in which eggs are boiled and the shells will not crack and let the whites leak out.

Mix one heaping pint of salt, a scant pint of lime, six quarts of water to make an excellent medium in which to store eggs.

In frying apples, add a small quantity of salt to make them "candy."

Soak green vegetables in salt water to remove insects, dirt, and other impurities.

As a cleanser for general household utilities, salt has so many applications that we can touch upon only a few of them:

When enamelled bathtubs and washbowls become yellow, rub with a solution of salt and turpentine to restore the whiteness.

Salt mixed with lemon juice cleans brass and other discolored metal.

Salt alone, rubbed on silver, brightens it. Rub silver with a cloth dipped in salt to remove egg stains.

Soot or oil stains on a carpet may be taken off by rubbing with salt. Several applications may be necessary.

A solution, equal parts of salt and pumice stone with enough water to make them adhere, is an effective cleansing wash for marble slabs—table tops, mantels and the like.

Bottoms of deep vases may be cleaned by allowing a solution of salt and vinegar to stand in them a short time and then rinsing with fresh water.

Rubbing the hands in salt removes the smell of gasoline. When you rub a spot off washable garments with gasoline, a "ring" is usually left. You can prevent that by washing the fabric in strong salt solution before cleaning.

Salt removes onion and/or perspiration stains from clothing.

Stains on earthenware and china disappear under a hard rubbing of salt.

To eliminate iron rust from cotton material, wet the spot with lemon juice, sprinkle it with salt, let it bleach in the sun.

Blood stains on cloth vanish when soaked in salt water, washed in warm water with plenty of soap and then boiled.

A good dry cleaner may be had by mixing equal parts of salt and cornmeal moistened with turpentine.

Colors in fabrics will not run, in washing, when salt is added to the water.

Soaking clothes for two hours in a pail of water to which one cup of salt has been added, sets the colors.

Clothes will not freeze when a large handful of salt is added to rinse water.

Soak clothespins in salt brine for a few hours and they will not stick to the clothes on the line.

A handful of salt in the rinse water prevents "bluing streaks."

To eliminate moths, sift dry salt over the carpet or rugs before cleaning.

Add a teaspoon of salt to the water in the goldfish bowl once a week; it invigorates your silent little pets.

Sweeping with a broom dipped in salt water keeps matting from turning yellow and gives it longer life.

Are you bothered with ants about the house? Sprinkle fine salt over the floors and shelves and watch them disappear.

When your flat iron gets rusty, rub it with wax; then scour it with salt.

Pouring salt brine once a week down the kitchen sink drain prevents grease from collecting and eliminates odors.

The kitchen table top can be whitened by washing it clean with soap and water, then rubbing with salt sprinkled plentifully on a cloth.

Glass globes and chimneys become gleaming white when rubbed with salt after washing.

Sometimes, in whitewashing walls, the new coating will not stick, but peels off. Adding a small quantity of salt to the whitewash before applying, corrects the trouble.

Adding a pinch of salt to water in a flower vase makes the blooms and leaves remain fresh for a longer time.

Then too, there are certain outdoor situations in which the use of salt proves advantageous:

A solution of one dram of salt, one ounce of water and two ounces of glycerin, effectually cleans the windshield on your car.

Sprinkle salt on the crevices of brick and cement walks to kill off weeds and grass.

Putting salt at the roots and stalk bases of weeds in the yard kills them off.

Salt also means death to poison ivy.

Ice on slippery front steps and walks melts when salt is sprinkled on it.

Placed in front of the rear wheels of a car stuck in the snow, salt melts the snow and permits the tire tread to get a purchase on the road.

And so on. Yes, salt is an excellent servant in the house and around the house.

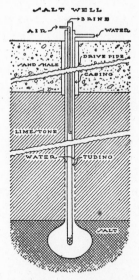

This drawing indicates the hydraulic system of obtaining brine from rock salt as developed on the principle first used by Geo. H. Smith in the 1880's. (See p. 167.)

And so we come to the end of our book about salt. We have seen how man, since before the time of written history, has realized his need for and his dependency upon "the fifth element;" has worked and planned and fought to have a sufficient and continuing supply.

For us present-day Americans, to know that we have just that, without the necessity of working, planning or fighting, is to pay tribute to the men who have made it possible. Pioneers, scientists, engineers, executives—men working at the wells, at the mines, at the solar ponds; in the plants and in the offices. All have contributed their meed of effort that now makes possible the vast American salt industry.

From Asa Danforth and Comfort Tyler, James Geddes and Moses DeWitt; from Tobias Ruffner and "Uncle" Billy Morris; from George Patrick and George Smith and Joseph Duncan and Joy Morton, and from hundreds of others as well, we profit today and acknowledge our debt.

It is with that thought in mind that the man who, as a boy, listened to the tales of old salt men and grew up to make a book about salt, expresses the hope you, in its perusal, have found something of entertainment and profit.

*

BIBLIOGRAPHY

Trans-Alleghany Pioneers, Dr. John P. Hale

History of Kanawha County, George W. Atkinson

Pages from the Past, George W. Summers

The Paths of Inland Commerce, Archer Butler Hulbert

The Springs of Virginia, Percival Reniers

Western Prices Before 1860, Thomas Senior Berry

The Story of the Confederacy, Robert S. Henry

Salt as a Factor in the Confederacy, Ella C. Lonn

History and Description of the Manufacture and Mining of Salt in New York State, Charles J. Werner

Syracuse and Its Environs, Franklyn H. Chase

The Texas Rangers, Walter Prescott Webb

The Pageant of the Packets, Garnett Laidlaw Eskew

Rock Salt, Its Origin, Gilbert Dennison Harris

The Covenant of Salt, Henry Clay Trumbull

An Excellent Treatise on Fire and Salt, Lord Blaise of Vigenere, 1649

Salt Deposits and the Salt Industry in Ohio, J. A. Bownocker

Salt Manual of the Saginaw Valley, Michigan, Alexander Winchell

In the Shadow of the Moroni, Charles A. Lucas

The Great Salt Lake, Dale Morgan

Bubbling Waters, Clarke B. Firestone

Studies in Administration and Finance, 1581-1825 (England), Edward Hughes

Salt and the Salt Industry (England), Albert F. Calvert

An Account of the Salt Springs of Salina, 1826, Lewis C. Beck

The Art of Making Common Salt, William Brownrigg, 1748

Transactions of the New York Agricultural Society, 1859, George Geddes

The Butter Industry, O. F. Hunziker

Keeping Livestock Healthy, U. S. Department of Agriculture

The Story of Food Preservation, Edith Elliot Swank

A Book for All Households or the Art of Preserving Animal and Vegetable Substances for Many Years, Nicolas Appert

Salt—Its Romantic History, Pamphlet Issued by the Worcester Salt Co.

The Present State of the Manufacture of Salt Explained, Earl of Dundonald, 1785

Descriptions of the Principles and Plan of Proposed Establishment of Salt Works, James Fennell, 1798

Artists' Manual, James Cutbush

Remarks of R. Hawley Before the Ways and Means Committee of the House of Representatives, 1872

The Australian Saltbush, Roland McKee

The Allegheny, Frederick Way

The Technology of Salt Making in the United States, W. C. Phalen

The Ethnography of Salt in Aboriginal North America, Helen Virginia Hunter (Thesis, Univ. of Pennsylvania)

Salt of the Frontier, Mary Hogue (Thesis, Univ. of Pittsburgh)

The Bible, and Various Bible Encyclopedias

Early American Archives

Back Files of:

    Syracuse (New York) *Herald*

    Charleston (West Virginia) *Gazette*

    Southern Cultivator

ACKNOWLEDGMENTS

Ed Tustin, public relations director, Worcester Salt Company, New York City, who placed at my disposal his wide knowledge of American salt history, with accompanying illustrative matter.

Katherine Sykora, whose assistance involved much more than the mere typing of this manuscript.

Charles C. Dickinson, Malden, W. Va., who shared with me his rich memories of salt making days in Kanawha, as heard from his father.

Major Harry C. Durston, secretary, Onondaga Historical Association, Syracuse, N. Y., for information on Syracuse's salty past.

Paul Payne, Public Librarian, Syracuse, N. Y., who told me more about Syracuse.

Ambrose I. Clayton, grandson of the great empire builder, Brigham Young, who steered me to where I could find invaluable material on Great Salt Lake.

Walter Koehler, president, Excelsior Salt Works, Pomeroy, Ohio, for accounts of the high old salt days in Pomory Bend.

William Smith, superintendent of Pomeroy Schools, for more of the same.

Ashton W. Reniers, cartographer of Kanawha, who read the first five chapters of this book and liked them.

The late Commodore F. A. Laidley, steamboat owner and salt maker, who learned the business, so to speak, from the ground up, and told me about it.

Dr. Temple Stalnaker, antiquarian and proprietor of the famous Rogers Drug Store, in Charleston, W. Va., for the use of his priceless historical collection.

Monroe Cockrell, for suggestions on Texas salt making.

Dr. Roy Bird Cook, historian, Charleston, W. Va.

Miss F. E. Harris, Bureau of Mines, U. S. Department of the Interior, for Commercial Statistics on salt.

Mrs. Willis Battaile and Mrs. Paul Porter of Washington, D.C., for directing me to sources of Kentucky's salt-making story.

Sterling Morton, whose memories of past salt production methods and personnel, no less than his ability as an editor, have added greatly to the production of this book.

Myron Sutton, Bill Langford and the other gentlemen of Saltair, Utah, for detailed description of solar salt making.

Messrs. Daniel Peterkin, Herbert Stratford, R. K. Warren, Carrington Clarke, E. R. Phillips, Jack McCune, Charles Gilpin, Bennett Carrington, Sid Carlson, Charles Flynn; and to Mrs. Margaret Conrad and Miss Bernice Kerr — all of the Morton Salt Company, for kindly and patient assistance in ways too numerous to mention.

The author wishes to acknowledge his indebtedness to Evva A. Brinker, Washington, D. C., for invaluable editorial and research assistance in the preparation of this volume.

INDEX

229